Priscilla Hauser's

decorative
PAINTING
1-2-3

Priscilla Hauser's

decorative PAINTING 1-2-3

Sterling Publishing Co., Inc.
New York

PROLIFIC IMPRESSIONS PRODUCTION STAFF:

Editor in Chief: Mickey Baskett
Copy Editor: Phyllis Mueller
Graphics: Dianne Miller, Karen Turpin
Photography: Jerry Mucklow
Administration: Jim Baskett

Library of Congress Cataloging-in-Publication Data Available

10 9 8 7 6 5 4 3 2 1

Published by Sterling Publishing Company, Inc.
387 Park Avenue South, New York, N.Y. 10016

Produced by Prolific Impressions, Inc.
160 South Candler St., Decatur, GA 30030

©2003 by Prolific Impressions, Inc.
Distributed in Canada by Sterling Publishing
c/o Canadian Manda Group, One Atlantic Avenue, Suite 105
Toronto, Ontario, Canada M6K 3E7
Distributed in Great Britain and Europe by Chrysalis Books,
64 Brewery Road, London N7 9NT, England
Distributed in Australia by Capricorn Link (Australia) Pty. Ltd.
P.O. Box 704, Windsor, NSW 2756 Australia

This book is dedicated to a wonderful group of women who made it happen, giving of their creative talents and time. Without them, this book would not have become a reality. They design, paint, teach, write, clean, sand, trim, and do anything that needs to be done. With love and thanks, I wish to acknowledge (alphabetically): Joyce Beebe, Alta Bradberry, Connie Deen, Jennifer Dunaway, Roseanne Mapp, Naomi Meeks, Sue Sensintaffar, Judy Kimball, and Barbara Sondrup.

ACKNOWLEDGEMENTS

Thanks to the following manufacturers for their support and for supplying product to use for the painting of the projects in this book:

Plaid Enterprises, Inc.
3225 Westech Dr.
Norcross, GA 30092
www.plaidonline.com
for FolkArt® Artists' Pigments™, FolkArt Acrylic Colors, FolkArt® painting mediums, Stamp Décor® stamps, Stencil Decor® Daubers, Spouncers®

Loew-Cornell
563 Chestnut Ave.
Teaneck, NJ 07666
www.loew-cornell.com
for artist paint brushes.

About Priscilla Hauser

She has been called "first lady of decorative painting" because of her early involvement in the teaching of the craft and her key role in organizing the first meeting of the National Society of Tole and Decorative Painters on October 22, 1972. Since that first meeting, attended by Priscilla Hauser and 21 others, the organization has thrived, and so has Priscilla.

From her beginning efforts as a tole painter in the early 1960s, when she took classes at a YMCA in Raytown, Missouri, Priscilla Hauser has become a world-renowned teacher and author and the decorative painting industry's ambassador to the world. She has traveled to teach in Canada, Japan, Argentina, and The Netherlands and has instructed extensively throughout the United States and at her Studio by the Sea in Panama City Beach, Florida. Besides teaching, Priscilla has illustrated her techniques through books, magazine articles, videos, and television. The results of her teaching program have led to an accreditation program for teachers.

Priscilla says to everyone, "I can teach you to paint. Come paint with me in my beautiful Studio by the Sea! You will learn the basics: brush strokes, double-loading, blending, and proper preparation of surfaces. You'll even learn some pen-and-ink techniques and some fabric painting." Priscilla's seminars are extremely valuable to beginners as well more advanced painters. Her methods teach the newcomer and strengthen the experienced. The seminars last five-and-a-half days and, after studying for 100 hours, you can become accredited with the Priscilla Hauser Program.

To receive seminar details, send for Priscilla Hauser's Seminar Brochure and Schedule, P.O. Box 521013, Tulsa, OK 75152-1013.

INTRODUCTION
Quick Fixes with Decorative Painting
page 9

PREPARING YOUR PROJECT
page 12

DECORATIVE PAINTING SUPPLIES
Paints, Mediums, Palette, Brushes, Other Supplies
page 14

BASIC INFORMATION
page 18

BRUSH SKILLS
Using a Round Brush, Using a Flat Brush,
Using a Liner Brush, Brush Stroke Worksheets
page 21

PAINTING TECHNIQUES
Floating Shading & Highlighting, Blending
page 24

PROJECTS
Lilac Cabinet
page 31

Dragonfly on Metal Ceiling Tile
page 44

Fish on a Tin Tub
page 48

Sunflowers Coat Rack
page 54

A Quick & Easy Leaf
page 64

Leaf Bordered Picture Frame
page 66

Blueberries Ensemble
page 70

Garden Window
page 80

Ladybug Garden Set
page 90

Seashells Headboard
page 96

Lemon Kitchen Shelf
page 106

Woodland Ferns Table
page 116

By the Sea Tray
page 126

Springtime Birdhouse Clock
page 135

Eat, Drink & Bee Merry Plate
page 140

Pyracantha Birdcage & Plant Stand
page 146

Holly Bucket
page 154

A special thanks to Summer House Village Antiques on Hwy. 98 in Inlet Beach, FL, for allowing us to shop, paint & photograph at their charming shops.

Traveling by car with my husband, Jerry, is an experience. I want to stop at every antique and "junktique" shop along the way to search for treasures. Jerry just wants to get to our destination! Occasionally, he gives in to my wishes, and we find wonderful things. These kinds of furniture treasures are perfect surfaces for decorative painting, and this book is full of painted projects to inspire you. And the wonderful thing about them is that many times you can use them "as is" with no additional preparation needed.

Since time is important to all of us, I look for pieces that don't require much preparation before the decorative painting is done. I often use the existing finish as my background, so just a little bit of sanding to smooth the old finish and a quick wipe with a tack cloth to remove excess dust or chipped paint is often all that is needed. The resulting surface has the aged, worn look

Quick Fixes with Decorative Painting

so popular today, and it's ready to paint.

Garage and tag sales are also wonderful sources of furniture pieces, and thrift stores and flea markets offer an abundance of furniture as well as decorative accessories. Many of the pieces I used for this book were found at a roadside antique shop in Panama City, Florida.

You can paint a piece and use it as a one-of-a-kind centerpiece or accent, or paint a number of pieces to make a coordinated grouping through the use of similar motifs.

One of my finds was a delicate little table, already painted white. To see how quickly and easily it was transformed into a painted treasure, turn to the "Blueberries" project on page 66. Chairs are everywhere, and I love to paint them. I painted a folding chair with blueberries to match the table, then painted a lamp to create a coordinated threesome.

Continued on next page

The whole idea is that your painting be quick and easy and effective. Perfection? Forget it! You are not striving for perfection, you're creating a look – a casual look, a comfortable look, and a look you can live with easily.

Let go – let your imagination run wild. If you see something you like, and if it is the right price, don't hesitate. Buy it! Take it home and have fun with it. You can do it in an afternoon.

Pictured clockwise from top: Seashells Headboard, Blueberries Chair, Blueberries Table – just a few "junktique" finds BEFORE their transformation into painted treasures.

Pictured at left: The Seashells Headboard AFTER painting.

Pictured below: The Blueberries Chair and Table AFTER painting.

Don't be afraid. Read the instructions, take brush in hand, and go for it. You're going to delight yourself with what you do. Remember – don't strive for perfection, just have fun!

PREPARING YOUR PROJECTS

The amount of preparation you do depends on the condition of the piece. For the projects in this book, I have used mostly old pieces that I found at flea markets. It is fun finding the perfect piece and transforming it from a "throwaway" into a treasure. New, unfinished wood furniture pieces can also be used to paint. I have included my tips for using both old and new pieces.

Old Pieces

If you are fortunate enough to find pieces that have already been painted and you like the color, it saves a tremendous amount of time. If the paint is in good condition, cleaning the piece with soap and water and allowing it to dry completely may be all that's needed.

If the paint is chipped or flaking, yet you want to keep the paint color and the old, distressed look, you will need to clean it and remove some of the chipped paint so that your new painting won't flake away. First sand the piece or scrap with a paint scraper to remove loose pieces of paint. You will want to do your decorative painting on top of a stable painted background. Wipe it with a tack cloth to remove the sanding dust. After just this small amount of prep work, you're ready to start your decorative painting.

If the paint cannot be rescued, if you don't like the color, or you don't want an aged look, a freshly painted basecoat may be required. Before you start, be sure the paint you apply is compatible with the type of paint you will use to do the decorative painting. If you are not sure, take a sample of your paint to a good paint store and ask them what type of paint you need for your basecoat.

Pictured above: *Sanding the existing finish on a blue-painted coat rack to remove loose and flaking paint.*

Here's how to apply a new basecoat:
1. Clean the surface.
2. Using a medium grade of sandpaper, sand the surface thoroughly.
3. Wipe with a tack cloth.
4. Apply a coat of stain blocker paint or gesso. Allow to dry thoroughly and sand again. Wipe with tack cloth.
5. Apply several coats of your desired basecoat color, sanding between coats.

CLEANING AN OLD PIECE

To remove dirt, dust, cobwebs, or grease, use a cleaner that does not leave a gritty residue. Effective cleaners include **mild dishwashing detergent** and **bubble bath**. Mix the cleaner with water and wash the furniture with a cellulose sponge. Rinse and wipe dry with soft cloth rags.

DISTRESSING PAINTED PIECES

Distressed finishes add the character imparted by use and age. You can create a simple distressed finish by scraping or sanding a painted piece to remove some of the paint, exposing layers of color (if there's more than one color of paint on the piece) and allowing some of the wood to show. This can be done with an old painted piece or a new piece that you have just painted. The best places to sand are those areas where age would be most apparent, such as edges and handles.

Sanding Tips:
- Sand more on the edges of the piece – concentrating your efforts in places where wear would normally occur over time – and less on flat areas for a more natural appearance.
- Don't use a sanding block or an electric sander – you want an uneven look. Holding the sandpaper in your hand is best and allows you more control.
- Use medium or medium-fine grit sandpaper to remove more paint, fine grit sandpaper to remove less.
- It's best to begin slowly and err on the side of removing too little paint rather than too much. You can always sand again to remove more. Stop when the result pleases you.

UNFINISHED WOOD PIECES

Preparation:
1. Sand piece thoroughly with medium, then with fine sandpaper. Wipe with a tack rag.
2. When using acrylic paints for basecoating a piece, it is usually not necessary to seal the wood. However, if there are knotholes or areas where wood is green, I apply a light coat of matte acrylic varnish to seal the flaw before applying paint. In general, however, I don't seal raw wood before painting because paint adheres better to unsealed wood.

Pictured above: *Lightly sanding a basecoated chair to give a distressed look.*

3. If the sealer has raised the grain of the wood, sand lightly with fine sandpaper. Wipe with a tack rag.

Different types of background treatments require different preparations. For example, if you are going to stain the piece, you will not need to seal the piece. Individual project instructions will tell what to do on the types of surfaces shown.

Basecoat Piece:

Basecoating is applying paint to a project surface you wish to decorate before the design is transferred to the surface.
1. With a sponge brush, apply a generous amount of paint. Let dry.
2. Sand with a piece of a brown paper bag with no printing on it to smooth the painted wood.
3. Apply a second coat of the base color, if needed for coverage. Let dry.
4. Use a piece of brown paper bag to smooth the surface again. (Sometimes a third coat of paint is necessary to achieve full coverage.)

Decorative Painting
SUPPLIES

PAINTS

The projects in this book were painted with **artist pigment acrylics**. These rich, creamy, opaque paints come in squeeze bottles and are available at art supply and craft stores. They have true pigment color names, just like oil paints. Their pigment is brilliant, and you can blend them and move them much in the same way as oil paints by using painting mediums.

Pre-mixed **acrylic craft paints** are available in hundreds of colors. These are not true pigment colors, but blended colors. They have the same consistency as artist's pigment acrylic paints and can be used for decorative painting the same way as artist's acrylic paints. In this book, I use them to undercoat designs and for basecoating. If you choose paints from the same manufacturer, you can be sure they will be compatible with one another.

MEDIUMS

Mediums are liquids or gels that are mixed with paint for achieving specific effects. They are sold along with the artist's acrylic paints. You will need floating medium and blending medium for each and every painting project.

Floating medium is used to thin the paint so that it can be used for floating a color. The brush is filled with the floating medium, a corner of the brush is then filled with color. After the brush is blended on the palette, the color is brushed along the edge of a design element to create a shading or highlighting. **Blending medium** is used to keep paint wet and moving. The medium is painted onto the surface in the area of the design where it is being painted. The design is painted immediately while the blending medium is still wet.

Glass and tile medium is used to make painting easier on slick surfaces. If you are painting on glass, metal, glazed ceramics, or candles – you will need this medium. It is painted onto the surface of the project, in the area where the design is going to be painted. After it has dried, the design is painted.

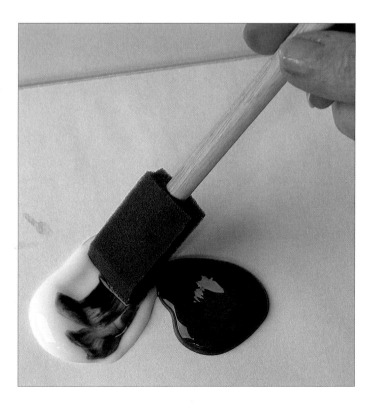

Glazing medium is used to thin the paint so that the mixture can be used as antiquing. The glazing medium is mixed with the paint on a palette or in a small container until a very thin transparent consistency is reached. This medium can also be used as a substitute for floating medium. It works in the same way.

When **textile medium** is mixed with paint before the paint is applied to cloth, the paint will be permanent on the fabric when it dries.

PALETTE

You will need a palette for all your painting projects. I like to use a "stay-wet" type palette. Some people prefer a wax-coated or dry palette for acrylics; however, I prefer a palette that stays wet since acrylics dry so quickly. Palettes can be found where decorative painting supplies are sold. A wet palette consists of a plastic tray that holds a wet sponge and special paper. To use palette:

1. Soak the sponge in water until saturated. Do not wring out, but place the very wet sponge into tray.

2. Soak the paper that comes with the palette in water for 12-24 hours. Place the paper on top of the very wet sponge.

3. Wipe the surface of the paper with a soft, absorbent rag to remove the excess water.

4. Squeeze paint on the palette. When paints are placed on top of a properly prepared wet palette, they will stay wet for a long time.

1. Soak the sponge in water until saturated.

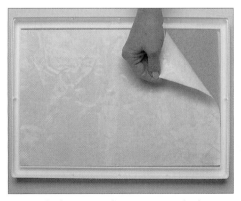

2. Soak the paper that comes with the palette.

3. Wipe the surface of the paper with a soft rag.

4. Squeeze paint on the palette.

BRUSHES

There are many different types of brushes, and different-shaped brushes do different things. You will need four types of brushes, in various sizes to do your decorative painting. The individual project instructions list the sizes of brushes needed for that particular project.

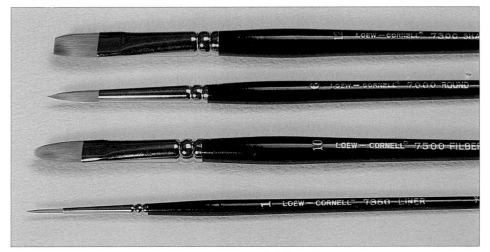

FLAT BRUSHES

Flat brushes are designed for brush strokes and blending. These brushes do most of the painting of the designs.

*Brush types, **pictured top to bottom**: flat, round, filbert, liner.*

ROUND BRUSHES

Round brushes are used primarily for stroking – we seldom blend with them. They can also be used for some detail work.

FILBERT BRUSHES

Filbert brushes are a cross between a flat and a round brush. They are generally used for stroking, but can also be used for blending.

LINER BRUSHES

Liner brushes are very thin round brushes that come to a wonderful point. Good liner brushes are needed for fine line work.

When it comes to brushes, please purchase the very best that money can buy. They are your tools – the things you paint with. Occasionally, a student says, "Priscilla, I don't want to buy a good brush until I know I can paint." I always tell my students they won't be able to paint if they don't begin with a good brush. You get what you pay for.

Brush strokes are the basis of my decorative painting technique. This book includes excellent brush stroke worksheets for practicing. To use them, lay a sheet of acetate or tracing paper over the top of the worksheets, choose a brush approximately the same size as the brush used on the worksheet, and practice hundreds of strokes on top of mine. (If a hundred sounds like a lot, get over it! You will find that painting a hundred strokes happens very quickly.)

BRUSH CARE

It's important to clean your brushes properly and keep them in excellent condition. To thoroughly clean them:

1. Gently flip-flop each brush back and forth in water until all the paint is removed, rinsing them thoroughly. Never slam brushes into a container and stir them. (**photo 1**)
2. Work brush cleaner through the hairs of the brush in a small dish and wipe the brush on a soft, absorbent rag. Continue cleaning until there is no trace of color on the rag. (**photo 2**)
3. Shape the brush with your fingers and store it so nothing can distort the shape of the hairs. Rinse the brush in water before using again.

Photo 1

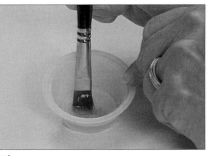

Photo 2

OTHER SUPPLIES

These are the basic supplies that are needed for each project. These are not listed in the individual project instructions; you will, however, need to gather them for each and every project.

Sandpaper - I use sandpaper for smoothing unfinished and finished wood surfaces and for creating a distressed, aged look on painted surfaces. Sandpaper comes in various grades from very fine to very coarse. It's good to keep a supply on hand.

Tack Rag - A tack rag is a piece of cheesecloth or other soft cloth that has been treated with a mixture of varnish and linseed oil. It is very sticky. Use it for wiping a freshly sanded surface to remove all dust particles. When not in use, store the tack rag in a tightly sealed jar.

Brown Paper Bags - I use pieces of brown paper bags with no printing on them to smooth surfaces after basecoating and between coats of varnish.

Tracing Paper - I like to use a very thin, transparent tracing paper for tracing designs. I use a **pencil** for tracing.

Chalk, White and Colored - I use chalk for transferring the traced design to the prepared painting surface. Chalk will easily wipe away and not show through the paint. This is why I prefer it to graphite paper. Do not buy the dustless kind.

Graphite Paper - Occasionally, I use white or gray graphite paper to transfer my design. However, I try to avoid using it because the lines may show through the paint. It can also make smudges on the background that are not easily removed.

Stylus - Use a stylus tool for transferring your traced design to the prepared surface. A pencil or a ballpoint pen that no longer writes also may be used.

Palette Knife - Use a palette knife for mixing and moving paint on your palette or mixing surface. I prefer a straight-blade palette knife made of flexible steel.

100% Cotton Rags - Use rags for wiping your brushes. *Here's a Tip: Use only 100% cotton rags for wiping your brush. Try the knuckle test: For 15 seconds, rub your knuckles on the rag that you wipe your brush on. If your knuckles bleed, think of what that rag is doing to the hairs of your brush!* You could also use soft, absorbent **paper towels** for wiping brushes.

Water Basin: Use a water basin or other container filled with water for rinsing brushes.

Varnish: See page 18, "Finishing Your Piece" for details.

BASIC INFORMATION

Transferring Patterns

TRANSFERRING A DESIGN WITH CHALK

1. Neatly trace the pattern of the design onto tracing paper. You may use a pencil or a pen. It is not necessary to trace shading lines or curlicues. (**photo 1**)
2. Turn over the traced design. Firmly go over the traced lines on the back with chalk. (**photo 2**) Do not scribble all over the tracing with the chalk.
3. Shake off the excess chalk dust, being careful not to inhale the particles.
4. Position the design on the prepared surface, chalk side down. Using a stylus, go over the lines. (**photo 3**) Don't press so hard that you make indentations in the surface. The chalk will be transferred to your surface. Chalk is easily removed and it dissolves as you paint over it.

Photo 1

TRANSFERRING A DESIGN WITH GRAPHITE

This technique is done the same way as the chalk technique. Instead of tracing over the back of the pattern with chalk, I trace over the back of the pattern with a #2 graphite pencil. I use this technique when transferring onto a very light surface where the chalk lines may not show, or the chalk lines won't be precise enough — such as for an inking technique. The graphite lines can be easily erased from the surface.

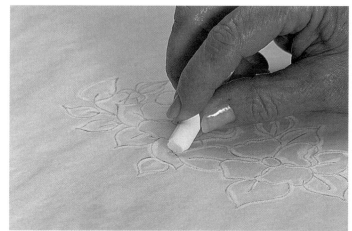

Photo 2

TRANSFERRING A DESIGN WITH TRANSFER PAPER

It is fine to transfer patterns onto a surface with white or gray transfer paper. However, this is my least favorite way to transfer a pattern because the transfer paper tends to smudge. To use transfer paper:

1. Trace pattern neatly and carefully from book onto tracing paper using a pencil or fine point marker. Enlarge or reduce the pattern on a copier if needed.
2. Position pattern onto surface. Secure one side with tape.
3. Slide the transfer paper under the pattern with the transfer side facing surface.
4. Using a stylus, neatly trace over pattern lines. This will transfer the lines to your surface.

Photo 3

Painting Tips

- When loading a brush with a different color, but one that is in the same color family, it is preferable to wipe the brush on a damp paper towel to remove excess paint before loading a new color. Avoid rinsing the brush too often in water.

- When loading your brush with a color in a different color family, the brush does not need to be thoroughly cleaned. Simply rinse in water and blot brush on a paper towel to remove excess water. Then load the brush with a new color.

- Sometimes I paint with a "dirty brush." Leaving some of the color in the brush from another element seems to blend the colors together better. For example, if I want to add a reddish tint to a leaf, I will leave a little green in my brush when I load the red so that the colors can "marry" together.

Flyspecking

Flyspecking adds an aged look to your pieces. To flyspeck a piece, you will need an old toothbrush, paint color of your choice, glazing medium, a palette knife, and a mixing surface such as a palette or a plastic container.

Photo 1: Add a small amount of paint color on your mixing surface. Add glazing medium to paint. Mix with palette knife to a very thin consistency. Dip toothbrush into the thinned paint.

Photo 2: Point the toothbrush at your surface and pull your thumb across the bristles to spatter the paint over the surface. You can also use the palette knife to pull across the surface of the toothbrush. The thinner the paint, the finer the spatter. Thicker paint will make larger spatters.

Finishing Your Piece

A clear finish is needed to protect the painted surface. For wood surfaces, I apply two or more coats of **waterbase varnish** as follows:

1. After the painting is thoroughly dry and cured, using a **synthetic bristle brush or a sponge brush**, apply a coat of brush-on varnish.

2. When the varnish is dry, rub the surface with a piece of a brown paper bag with no printing on it to smooth the surface.

3. Apply a final coat of varnish or a coat of clear **paste wax**.

Painting Terms

BASECOATING
Preparing and painting your project surface before the decorative painting is applied.

BASIC BRUSH STROKES
Basic brush strokes are done with round and flat brushes. Brush strokes are like the letters of the alphabet. They are easy to learn, but they do require practice. Learning these are very important as they are the basis for all of your painting. For example, if you are painting a flower petal, such as a daisy, paint each petal with one brush stroke such as a teardrop. Use as few strokes as possible to paint each part of the design.

COLOR WASH
A color wash is an application of very thin paint. Actually, one could say it is water with just a little color in it that is applied over a painted surface to add a blush of color. A wash can also be made with glazing medium and a bit of color.

CONSISTENCY
Consistency describes the thickness or thinness of the paint. You need different consistencies for different techniques. When you do brush strokes, the paint must be a creamy consistency. When you do line work, the paint must be very thin like the consistency of ink. If the paint is too thick, add a few drops of water to the paint puddle on your palette and mix with a palette knife until the proper consistency is reached.

CONTRAST
Contrast is the sharp difference between two or more colors. When two colors meet, one edge must be light (usually the top edge) and the other edge or shadowed area must be dark. Contrast gives life to your painting.

CURING
When something is dry to the touch, it is not cured. If something is cured, it is dry all the way through. I often explain curing with this analogy: If you fall down and skin your knee and it bleeds, it's wet. When the scab forms, it's dry. When the new skin grows, it's cured.

I am frequently asked how long it takes a painted piece to cure. There is no right answer – curing depends upon the temperature, air circulation, humidity, the paint color used, and the thinness or thickness of the paint. When a piece is cured, it feels warm and dry to the touch. Curing can take three hours or several weeks.

DOUBLE-LOADING
Double-loading is a technique of loading the brush with two colors of paint. Using two different puddles of paint, load half of the brush with the lighter color and the other half with the darker color. Blend by stroking your brush many, many times on the palette on one side of the brush, then turn the brush over and stroke on the other side. It takes many strokes to prime a brush and get it good and full of paint.

OUTLINING
Most of the time, I outline with a #1 liner brush. (It's possible to outline with the very fine point of any good brush.) When outlining, the brush should be full of paint that has been thinned to the consistency of ink.

STIPPLING
To stipple you will need a stippling brush, a scruffy brush or a stencil brush. These brushes have a flat tip. Brush is loaded, then dabbed up and down on the surface to produce an irregular covering of paint. The paint is applied in little dots or specks from the flat brush tip.

UNDERCOATING
Undercoating is neatly and smoothly painting a design or part of a design solidly on the basecoated project surface. Your strokes, shading, and highlighting will be done on top of this undercoated design.

WASH
See "Color Wash."

BRUSH SKILLS

Using a Round Brush

Round brushes are used primarily for stroking – we seldom blend with them. They come in a variety of sizes. Practice your round brush strokes on the Brush Stroke Worksheets.

LOADING THE BRUSH

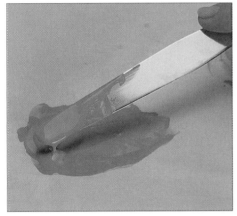

Photo 1. Squeeze paint onto your palette. If needed, thin your paint with a thinning medium such as glazing medium or water. Paint should be a creamy consistency.

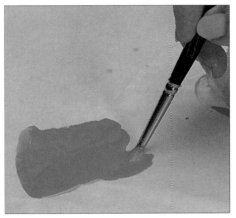

Photo 2. Load brush by picking up paint from the edge of the puddle.

TEARDROP OR POLLIWOG STROKE

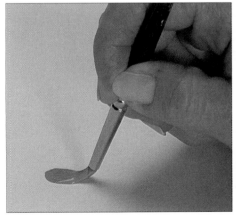

Photo 1. Touch on the tip of the brush and apply pressure.

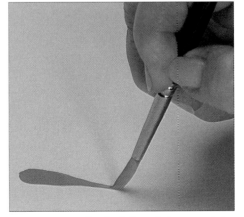

Photo 2. Gradually lift and drag straight down. Turning the brush slightly left or right forces the hairs back together to form a point.

BRUSH STROKE TIPS

- For brush strokes, the paint should have a thin, flowing consistency.

- Be sure your brush is full with paint so you don't run out of paint mid-stroke.

- While I don't deliberately get paint up in the ferrule, I don't worry about it. If you clean your brush properly, you will have no problems.

- Always use a fine brush in excellent condition. Choose brushes from a quality manufacturer that stands behind its products.

- Make a flag with a piece of tape on the handle of the paintbrush. When painting strokes, with the exception of the half-circle stroke, the flag should not wave, and you should not twist the brush in your fingers. You simply touch, press, pull, and lift. When you paint the half-circle stroke, the brush is pivoting in your fingers.

Using a Flat Brush

Flat brushes are designed for brush strokes and blending. They come in many different sizes. Flat brush strokes or any type of stroke may be painted in a single color. It is always a good idea to practice the stroke using a single color before you double-load. These photos show the brush being double-loaded. The procedure is the same if you are using a single color. Practice your flat brush strokes on the Brush Stroke Worksheets that follow.

DOUBLE-LOADING

Double-loading involves loading your brush with two colors. Be sure to thin paint with water to a flowing consistency and push it with a palette knife to form a neat puddle with a clean edge.

Photo 1. Stroke up against the edge of the light color 30 times, so half of the brush is loaded with paint and the other half is clean.

Photo 2. Turn the brush over and stroke up against the edge of the dark color 20 times.

Photo 3. Blend, blend, blend one side of the brush on your palette.

Photo 4. Turn the brush over and blend, blend, blend on the other side, keeping the dark color in the center and the light color to the outside.

Photo 5. Go back and pick up more light paint on the brush.

Photo 6. Go back to the blending spot on your palette and blend some more.

Photo 7. Go back and pick up some more of the dark color.

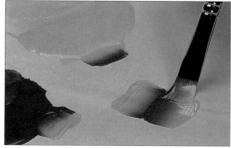

Photo 8. Go back to the blending spot on your palette and blend some more. Continue doing this until your brush is really full with paint.

Photo 9. Here is a correctly double-loaded brush. You don't want a space between the two colors; you want them to blend into each other in the center of the brush.

LINE STROKE

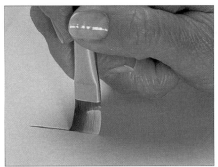

Stand the brush on its flat or chisel edge, perpendicular to the orientation of the basic flat stroke. The handle should point straight up toward the ceiling. Pull the brush toward you. Don't press the brush down, as this will thicken and distort the line.

BASIC STROKE

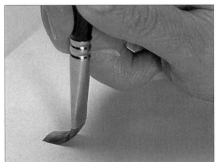

Photo 1. Touch the length of the flat or chisel edge of the brush to your surface.

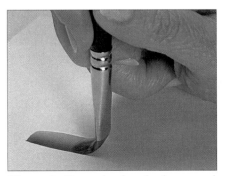

Photo 2. Press the brush down and pull it toward yourself, holding the pressure steady. Lift the brush smoothly at the end of the stroke.

Using a Liner Brush

Liner brushes are the long, thinner members of the round brush family. The bristles come to a wonderful point. Liner brushes are used for fine line work. Practice your liner brush strokes on the Brush Stroke Worksheets.

LOADING

Photo 1. Thin paint with water until it is the consistency of ink.

Photo 2. Fill the brush full of paint by pulling it through paint. Twist brush as you pull it out of puddle. this will form a nice pointed tip. When you are using the brush hold it straight up.

TEARDROP STROKE

Fill brush with paint of a thin consistency; touch, apply pressure, begin pulling and lifting, then drag to a point.

CURLICUES & SQUIGGLES

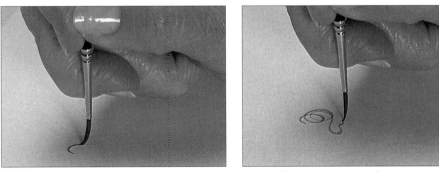

Photo 1. Stand the brush on its point with the handle pointing straight up toward the ceiling.

Photo 2. Slowly move the brush to paint loopy Ms and Ws. Practice several times on your page. Make as many variations as you wish.

Round Brush Strokes

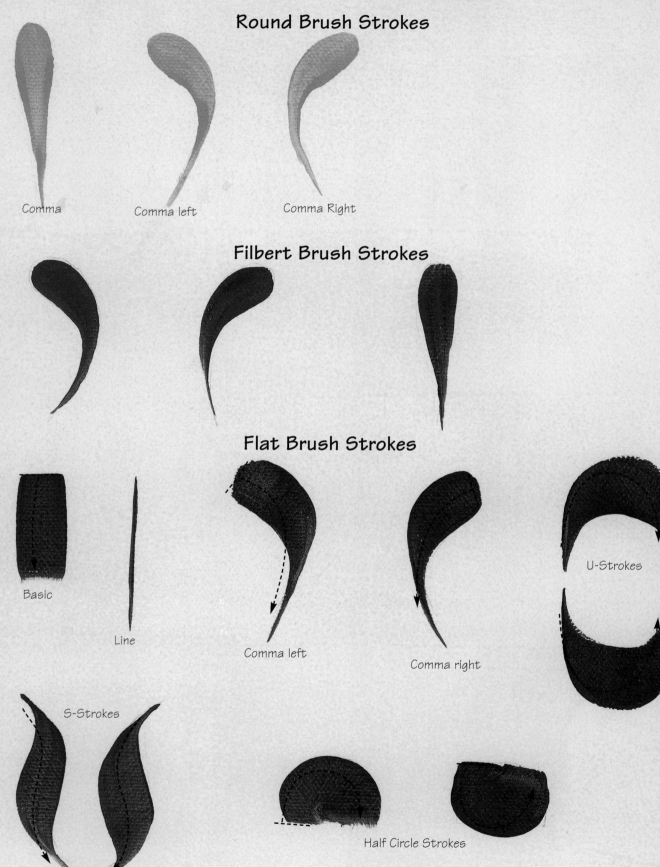

Comma

Comma left

Comma Right

Filbert Brush Strokes

Flat Brush Strokes

Basic

Line

Comma left

Comma right

U-Strokes

S-Strokes

Half Circle Strokes

Double-Loaded Brush Strokes (using a #12 flat brush)

Basic

Line

Comma left

Comma right

U-Strokes

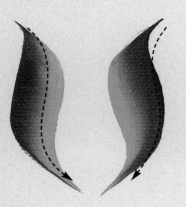

S-Strokes

Half Circle Strokes

Liner Brush Strokes

Use a very thin paint and a full brush. Move the brush slowly.

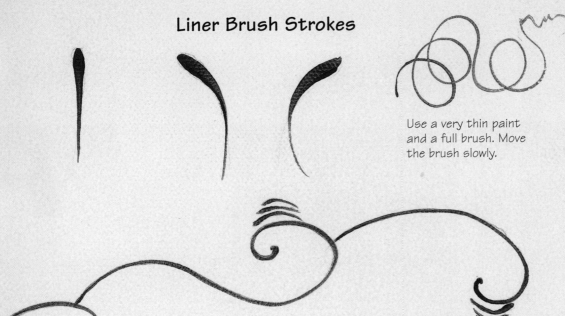

PAINTING TECHNIQUES

Shading & Highlighting with Floating Technique

Floating is flowing color on a surface. This technique is used for adding the shading and highlighting to design elements. Before floating, undercoat the area with a base color. Let dry. Add a second or even a third coat, if necessary. Let dry. Our example will show the shading and highlighting being floated onto a leaf that has been undercoated in a Bayberry color. Floating medium, glazing medium, or water can be used with the paint.

Photo 1. Fill as large a brush as you can possibly use on the area with floating medium.

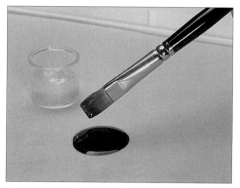

Photo 2. Fill one side of the brush with the shading color by stroking up against the edge of a puddle of paint.

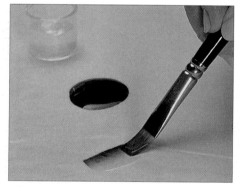

Photo 3. On a matte surface, such as tracing paper or wet palette paper, blend, blend, blend on one side of the brush.

Photo 4. Turn the brush over and blend, blend, blend on the other side. Keep paint in the center. The color should graduate through the brush from dark to medium to clear.

Photo 5. The floating of the shading and highlighting will be done atop the undercoating. Here the leaf has been undercoated with Bayberry.

Photo 6. Float on the shading to the edge of the design (leaf). Have the dark side of the brush towards the outside of the design. Let dry. Repeat the process, if desired, to deepen the color.

Photo 7. Highlighting is floated on the opposite side of the design. Highlighting is done using same technique as shading – but done with a light color.

Option: Water can be used in place of Floating Medium. Blot brush on edge of basin.

Blending

In this book, I have done a very easy type of blending. First, neatly and carefully undercoat the design area with paint and let dry. Blending Medium is used for this technique. It will allow you to blend colors together.

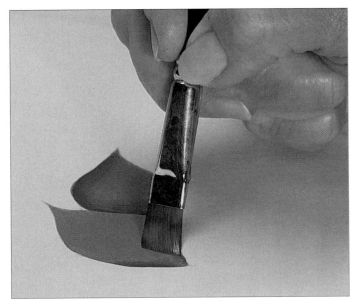

Photo 1. Float on the shadows. Let dry.

Photo 2. Add a small amount of blending medium to the design area.

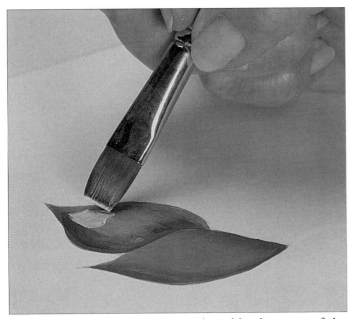

Photo 3. Add the colors you wish to blend on top of the wet medium.

Photo 4. Lightly blend or move the colors together, using an extremely light touch. If you are heavy handed, you will wipe all the color away. If this happens, let the blending medium dry and cure and begin again *or* remove the color before it dries, add more blending medium, and begin again.

28

PROJECTS
to Complete
in an Afternoon

Now it's time to paint. This section includes instructions for projects on a variety of surfaces. Each project includes a listing of the paint colors and supplies, painting worksheets that illustrate the techniques, and step-by-step instructions for preparing, painting, and finishing.

For all projects, in addition to the supplies listed with the individual project instructions, you will need to have these supplies on hand:

Sandpaper, in various grades from very fine to very coarse.

Tack rag, for wiping sanded surfaces.

Pieces of brown paper bags, without printing on them, to smooth surfaces between coats of paint or varnish.

Tracing paper, for tracing designs.

A pencil, for tracing.

Chalk, white and colored, for transferring the traced designs.

Graphite paper, white and gray, for transferring designs.

Eraser, for removing graphite transfer lines from surface.

A stylus, pencil, or ballpoint pen that no longer writes, for transferring the traced designs.

Palette, for placing paint.

Palette knife, for mixing and moving paint on your palette or mixing surface.

100% cotton rags, for wiping your brushes or wiping surfaces.

Water basin, for rinsing brushes.

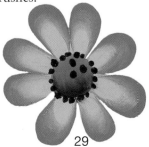

Lilac Cabinet

Lilacs are a favorite of mine to paint and to smell. This design flows beautifully on the front of any cabinet or vertical piece.

Lilacs, geraniums, and hydrangeas are examples of clump flowers. Quick and easy to paint, they are comprised of a multitude of little four-petal flowers. On the Lilac Worksheet, you will see how I press on the brush and pull and lift to create the little petal-strokes.

PALETTE OF COLORS

Artist Pigment Acrylic Paints:

Green Dark

Green Light

Green Umber

Payne's Gray

Prussian Blue

Pure Black

Pure Magenta

Titanium White

Yellow Light

Ice Blue (mix)

Acrylic Craft Paints:

Light Periwinkle

Old Ivy

Pure Gold (metallic)

BRUSHES

Flats - #2, #10, #12

Liner - #1

1" bristle brush

Sponge brush for painting surface

SURFACE

Wooden cabinet, unfinished or flea market find

OTHER SUPPLIES

In addition to the Basic Supplies listed on page 29, you will need:

Blending medium

Waterbase varnish

Latex wall paint in eggshell finish for painting cabinet: White

Instructions follow on page 33.

PREPARATION

1. Sand the surface, if needed. Wipe with a tack cloth.
2. Paint the panels where the lilacs will be painted with Periwinkle acrylic craft paint.
3. Paint the rest of the chest with white latex wall paint. Let dry. Apply a second coat, if needed.
4. Sand and wipe with a tack cloth.
5. Neatly trace and transfer the design using white graphite or chalk.

PAINTING THE DESIGN

See the Lilac Worksheet and the step-by-step photos that follow before you start to paint.

Leaves:

1. Neatly undercoat with two or more coats of Old Ivy, letting the paint dry between each coat.
2. Apply Green Umber + Payne's Gray (1:1) at the base of the leaf to create the shadow. Let dry.
3. Apply blending medium. Apply more of the shadow color – a little Green Dark, Green Light, and some Titanium White. Wipe the brush. Blend.

Lilacs:

Please notice the irregular shape of the lilac clump on the Lilac Worksheet – see how scattered the flowers are. Don't place them too close together. Practice making the little flowers several times before you actually paint on your prepared surface. See the illustration at the bottom of the Lilac Worksheet.

1. Apply blending medium to the lilac clump.
2. Apply Green Light at the top of the clump, then Pure Magenta and Prussian Blue. The blending medium will keep the paint wet, but since you are using acrylics, you need to work quickly.
3. Fill the #2 flat brush with Prussian Blue and wipe it on a rag. Make the four petal strokes that form the back or shadow flowers.
4. Wipe the brush. Pick up a small amount of Titanium White. Make more flowers – medium value ones – on top of the shadow flowers. The wet color underneath will shade the little flowers.
5. Wipe the brush and add two or three more flowers – very white ones – to create the top layer.

Centers:

Using your liner with thinned Yellow Light and Pure Black (each thinned to an ink-like consistency with water), apply a tiny dot of each color side-by-side on just a few lilacs. Let dry.

FINISHING

1. Trim the chest with Pure Gold, using the photo as a guide. Let dry.
2. Apply two or more coats of waterbase varnish. Let dry thoroughly. ❑

Painting a Leaf

1. Neatly undercoat the leaf with two or more coats Old Ivy. Let the paint dry between each coat.

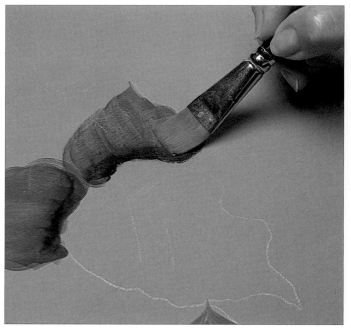

2. Apply Green Umber + Payne's Gray (1:1) at the base of the leaf to create the shadow. Let dry.

3. Apply blending medium to the entire leaf.

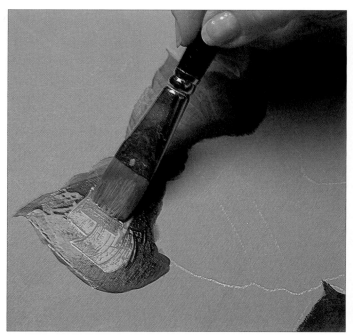

4. Apply leaf colors over the blending medium – a little Green Dark, a little Green Light, and some Titanium White.

5. Wipe the brush and blend the colors.

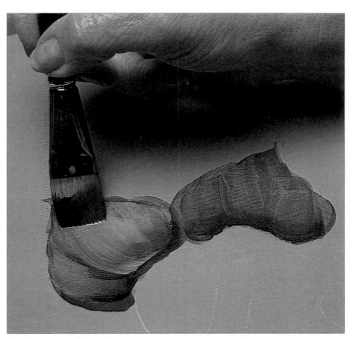

6. Continue blending.

How to Paint Lilacs

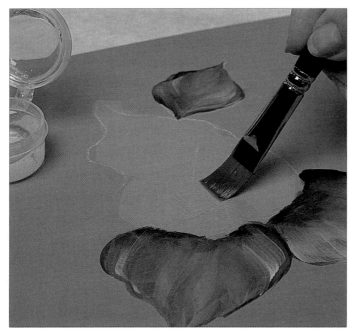

1. Apply blending medium to the lilac clump.

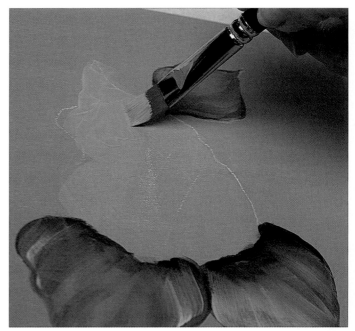

2. Apply Green Light at the top of the clump.

3. Then apply Pure Magenta and Prussian Blue. The blending medium will keep the paint wet, but since you are using acrylics, you need to work quickly.

4. Fill the #2 flat brush with Prussian Blue and wipe it on a rag. Make the four petal strokes that form the back or shadow flowers.

5. Wipe the brush. Pick up a small amount of Titanium White. Make more flowers – medium value ones – on top of the shadow flowers. The wet color underneath will shade the little flowers.

6. Wipe the brush and add two or three more flowers – very white ones – to create the top layer.

7. Add the center dots with Yellow Light and Pure Black (each thinned to an ink-like consistency with water), using liner brushes, on just a few lilacs. Let dry.

Lilacs Worksheet

Fig. 1
Undercoat leaf with Old Ivy. Let dry.

Hauser Green Light

Pure Magenta

Shadow Green Umber + Payne's Gray 1:1

Prussian Blue

Apply blending medium, then colors.

Fig. 2
Apply blending medium to leaf. Stroke on Green Umber. Add Titanium White.

Using a #2 flat, paint shadow flowers with blending medium and Prussian Blue.

Titanium White

Hauser Green Light

Fig. 4
Blend.

Add centers of Yellow Light and Pure Black dots.

Add just a few light value flowers.

Fig. 3
Stroke on medium value flowers.

39

Dragonfly on Metal Ceiling Tile

If you dig just a little, perhaps you'll find marvelous old ceiling tiles in one of those magical roadside antique shops. If you cannot find an old one, wonderful reproductions can be found in craft stores.

Do you know the legend of the dragonfly? Their mystical powers bring luck to all. I enjoy painting them in metallic colors. Using a round sponge brush (the kind sold for stenciling) makes it easy to paint circles.

PALETTE OF COLORS

Acrylic Craft Paints:

Blue Sapphire (metallic)

Licorice

Peridot (metallic)

Pure Gold (metallic)

Real Brown

Solid Bronze (metallic)

Wicker White

Hologram Sparkle

BRUSHES
Flats - #2, #4, #8
Liner - #1
Round sponge brush, 1/4"

SURFACE
12" metal ceiling tile

OTHER SUPPLIES
In addition to the Basic Supplies listed on page 29, you will need:
Blending medium
Waterbase varnish, gloss sheen

If you're using a new tile:
Aerosol metal primer
White vinegar or rubbing alcohol

PREPARATION

For an old tile:
1. Sand with fine grade sandpaper to remove any loose or chipping paint.
2. Paint the center square and the trim areas on the tile with two or more coats of Real Brown. Allow the paint to dry between coats.
3. Neatly trace and transfer the pattern.

For a new tile:
1. Wash with detergent or in the dishwasher. Dry thoroughly.
2. Wipe with white vinegar or alcohol.
3. Spray with a good metal primer (these come in a multitude of colors). You can apply a basecoat color on top of the metal primer or do the decorative painting directly on the primer.

continued on page 46, see page 43 for pattern

PAINTING THE DESIGN

See the Dragonfly Worksheet.

Wings:

1. Apply a small amount of blending medium to the wings, working one section at a time.
2. Double-load a brush with blending medium and Pure Gold. Apply the color around the outside edges of the wings. Wipe the brush.
3. Pull just a little of the color down toward the body. Let dry.
4. Shade the wings where they touch the back of the dragonfly with a little bit of Licorice, floating the color on. Let dry. **Option:** Apply a little blending medium to the dried wings, add a tiny touch of Licorice, and then pull the color into the wings. Let dry.
5. Wash wings with Hologram sparkle paint.

Head & Body:

Practice using the round sponge brush on a brown piece of paper before doing your painting. **Option:** Paint the circles with a small flat brush.

1. Dip the round sponge brush in Sapphire. Blot on a rag. Paint the head. Two or more coats may be needed to cover. Clean the round sponge brush.
2. Dip the round sponge brush in Peridot. Paint the circles that form the body. Two or more coats may be needed to cover. Let dry.
3. Shade the head with Licorice: Pick up a tiny bit of Licorice on the side of the round sponge brush, press, and lift. Clean the sponge brush.
4. Highlight the head with Wicker White: Touch the edge of the round sponge brush in Wicker White, blot, press, and lift.
5. Using the same technique, shade the body with Solid Bronze, then Licorice.

Antennae & Legs:

1. Thin Pure Gold to an ink-like consistency with water.
2. Fill a #1 liner brush with the thinned paint and carefully paint the antennae and legs. Let dry.

Grass & Flowers:

1. Paint the grass, using long, graceful strokes of Peridot, Solid Bronze, and Pure Gold.
2. Paint the little flowers with Wicker White.

Leaf Border:

1. Paint leaves, following the leaf instructions for project titled "Leaf Bordered Picture Frame." Add a touch of Peridot to the leaves, if desired.
2. Paint the berries with Pure Gold. Let dry and cure.

FINISHING

Varnish with three coats of high gloss waterbase varnish or other varnish of your choice. ❑

Dragonfly Worksheet

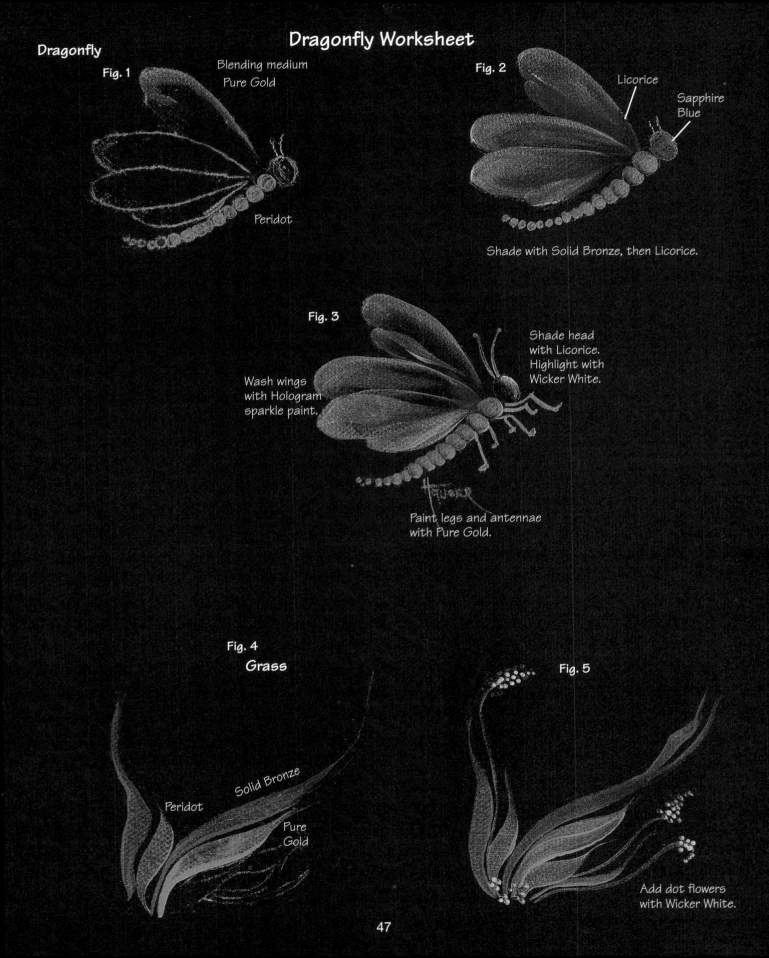

Dragonfly

Fig. 1

Blending medium
Pure Gold

Peridot

Fig. 2

Licorice

Sapphire
Blue

Shade with Solid Bronze, then Licorice.

Fig. 3

Wash wings
with Hologram
sparkle paint.

Shade head
with Licorice.
Highlight with
Wicker White.

Paint legs and antennae
with Pure Gold.

Fig. 4
Grass

Peridot

Solid Bronze

Pure
Gold

Fig. 5

Add dot flowers
with Wicker White.

Fish on a Tin Tub

*This old galvanized tub is one of my favorite pieces – I added a sponged back-ground and painted it with delightful tropical fish. I hope you enjoy painting fish as much as I did. Try them in any and all colors you desire.
I chose colors that are bright and happy.*

This tub is shown filled with picnic plates and cold drinks, but its uses are endless. It's a wonderful way to decorate for a backyard, beach, or garden party, and it would also be an excellent serving container for shrimp.

PALETTE OF COLORS

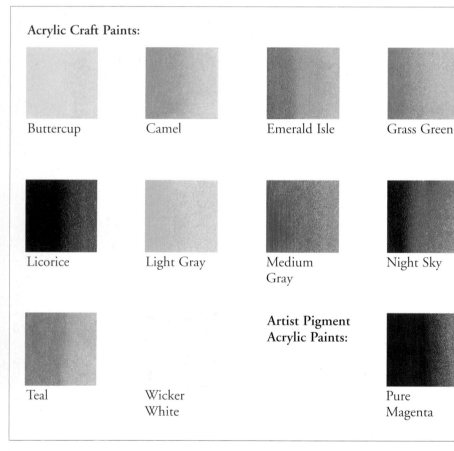

Acrylic Craft Paints:

Buttercup   Camel   Emerald Isle   Grass Green

Licorice   Light Gray   Medium Gray   Night Sky

Teal   Wicker White

Artist Pigment Acrylic Paints:

Pure Magenta

BRUSHES
Flats - #2, #10, #12
Liner - #1, #2

SURFACE
Galvanized tub, 21" long x 7" high

OTHER SUPPLIES
In addition to the Basic Supplies listed on page 29, you will need:

Blending medium

Sea sponge

Acrylic spray sealer

PREPARATION

1. Wash the galvanized tub with soap and water. Wipe dry and place in the oven on low setting for a few hours or allow to dry for several days.
2. Wipe the tub with rubbing alcohol.
3. Using the sponge, apply Camel, then Buttercup, then Wicker White to the design area. Pounce with the sponge to mingle the colors. Refer to the photos that follow and the Fish Worksheet to see how this was done.
4. Sponge the rim in the same manner, using the same colors. Allow to dry thoroughly.
5. Trace and transfer the outline of the fish and seaweed.

PAINTING THE DESIGN

See the Fish Worksheet.

Fish:

1. Prepare a gray mixture of Light Gray + Medium Gray (1:1).
2. Using a flat brush, undercoat the fish body with two coats of the gray mixture.
3. Undercoat the fins with one coat of the gray mixture.
4. Shade the top of the body and the lower fins with a Licorice float.
5. Highlight the base of the body with a Warm White float. Let dry.
6. Transfer the interior design lines to the fish.
7. Using a #2 liner brush, paint Warm White lines on the body and tail.
8. Shade the top of the body again with a Licorice float. Create the fin on the side of the body with Licorice.
9. Using a #1 liner brush, paint the gill line, the lines in the fins, and the mouth with Licorice thinned to an ink-like consistency.
10. Wash over the fish with the color or colors of your choice; Pure Magenta, Night Sky, and Teal are shown on the Fish Worksheet. (A "wash" is the application of a thin coat of color – to make a wash, mix 5 parts water to 1 part color.)
11. Re-shade with Licorice and re-highlight with Wicker White as needed.
12. Highlight the fins and tail with Wicker White line work.

Eye:

1. Using the handle end of a large brush, touch on a large dot of thinned Wicker White. Let dry.
2. Touch on a smaller dot of thinned Licorice. Allow to dry.

3. Apply a wash of Licorice over the white of the eye.

4. With a stylus, add a tiny highlight of thinned Wicker White.

Seaweed:

1. Using the #2 liner brush, paint with Grass Green. Let dry.

2. Accent with a wash of Emerald Isle.

FINISHING

1. Apply a Grass Green wash to the painted rim of the tub. Allow to dry completely.

2. Spray well with varnish. Let dry. ❑

Sponging the Background

1. Load sponge with one paint color. Dip the sponge in the paint, then dab on a clean part of the palette.

2. Sponge the first color on the surface.

3. Load the second color on the dirty sponge.

4. Sponge the second color on the surface. Repeat the process with the third color. Pounce the surface with the dirty sponge to mingle the colors.

Fish Worksheet
Fish

Background :
Sponge with Camel, Buttercup, and Wicker White.

Fig. 1
Undercoat with gray mix (Light Gray + Medium Gray 1:1). Apply 2 coats on body and tail, 1 on fins.

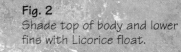

Fig. 2
Shade top of body and lower fins with Licorice float.

Fig. 3
Highlight bottom of body with Wicker White float. Transfer pattern.

Fig. 4
Paint Wicker White stripes on body and tail.

Eye

○ Wicker White dot

◉ Licorice dot

◉ Wash with Licorice. Add Wicker White dot.

Fig. 5
Shade top of body and create fin with Licorice. Add Licorice line work.

Fig. 6
Pink Fish: Wash with Pure Magenta. Reinforce shading and highlighting.

Paint seaweed with Grass Green.

Fig. 7
Purple Fish: Wash with Night Sky. Reinforce shading and highlighting.

Fig. 8
Turquoise Fish: Glaze with Teal. Reinforce shading and highlighting.

Accent seaweed with Emerald Isle.

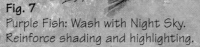

Fish Pattern
Enlarge @145%

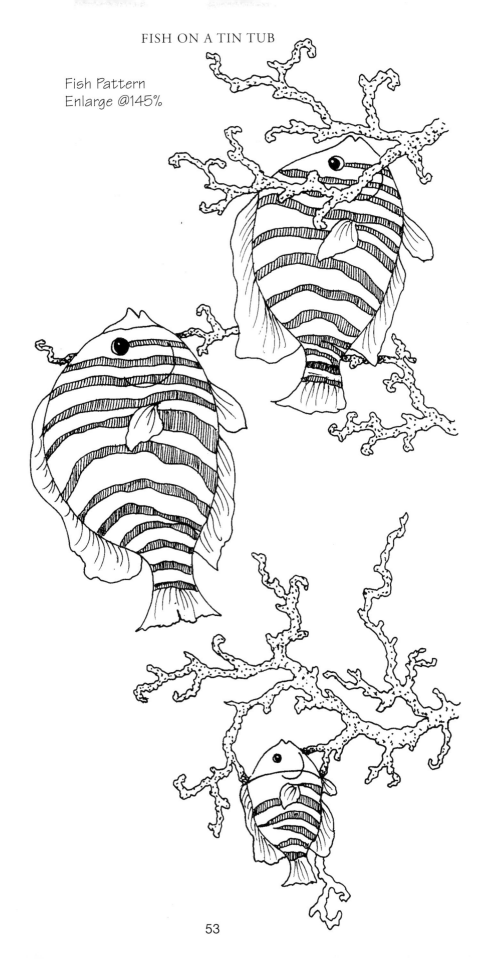

Sunflowers Coat Rack

I found this interesting piece of wood, but I don't know its origin – maybe it was a panel from a piece of furniture or a shutter. When I saw it, I knew I wanted to screw coat hooks into it and paint sunflowers on it. The beautiful, rich teal color is original, and the paint has been worn off and cracked beautifully by time.
I love it!

You could paint this design on any panel or shutter of your choice. Find coat hooks at hardware stores and home improvement centers.

Instructions follow.

PALETTE OF COLORS

Artist Pigment Acrylic Paints:

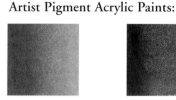   

Burnt Sienna	Burnt Umber	Green Dark	Green Light

Green Umber	Medium Yellow	Pure Orange	Red Light

Turner's Yellow	Yellow Ochre

Acrylic Craft Paints:

Clover	Lemon Custard	Pure Gold (metallic)	Warm White

BRUSHES

The brushes you use depend upon the size of sunflower you paint. I used these:

Flats - #14, #16, #20

Liner - #1

Watercolor brush - #3 round

Old scruffy brush or stencil brush (for stippling the flower center)

Old toothbrush (for flyspecking)

SURFACE

Wooden panel, approx. 11" x 36", painted dark turquoise

Metal hooks for coats

OTHER SUPPLIES

In addition to the Basic Supplies listed on page 29, you will need:

Blending medium

Floating medium

Waterbase varnish, satin or gloss

CAUTION!

Old paint can contain lead. Always be aware of this when working with an old painted surface.

- Carefully discard the residue of **any** old paint.

- Wearing a respirator is a good idea when sanding an old painted piece.

PREPARATION

If you are fortunate enough to find an old, peeling panel like I did:

1. Sand with fine grade sandpaper to remove any cracking or flaking pieces of paint.
2. Wipe with a tack cloth.

PAINTING THE DESIGN

Leaves:

1. Using a large flat brush, neatly undercoat the leaves with Pure Gold. (Pure Gold is a little more opaque than some acrylic paints and will help you obtain better coverage.) Let dry. Apply a second coat and a third coat of Pure Gold, as needed. Let dry between coats. Let cure.
2. Neatly undercoat with Clover. Let dry. Apply a second coat and a third coat, if needed.
3. Finish painting the leaves, following the instructions and examples for "Painting a Quick & Easy Leaf," as shown on pages 60-61.

Sunflower:

See the Sunflower Worksheet.

1. Using a large flat brush, neatly undercoat the sunflower with several coats of Pure Gold. Let the paint dry between each coat. Let cure.
2. Stroke the petals with Lemon Custard. Several coats will be needed to cover. Let dry.
3. Paint a few of the petals with Turner's Yellow and a few with Yellow Ochre (these are the back petals). Use an S-stroke to paint each half of each petal.
4. Paint the rest of the petals with Medium Yellow.
5. Using an old scruffy brush (such as an old stencil brush), dab (stippling) a little Burnt Sienna around the center and slightly on the petals.
6. Wipe the brush on a rag. Pick up a little bit of Red Light. Dab the Red Light over the Burnt Sienna.
7. Add highlighting to petal tips using a Medium Yellow float.

8. Using the same brush, dab Burnt Umber in the center. Let some of the gold show through.
9. To highlight the center, dab on Medium Yellow, Yellow Ochre, Pure Orange, and Red Light.

Bud:

See the Sunflower Bud Worksheet.

1. Undercoat with Pure Gold. Several coats will be needed to cover. Let the paint dry between coats. After last coat, let dry and cure.
2. Apply several coats of Lemon Custard to the petals. Let dry.
3. Paint a few of the petals with Turner's Yellow and a few with Yellow Ochre (these are the back petals).
4. Paint the rest of the petals with Medium Yellow.
5. Using the old scruffy brush, dab a little Burnt Sienna at the base of the petals. Let dry.
6. Undercoat the calyx and stem with several coats of Clover. Let the paint dry between each coat.
7. Paint the individual "petals" of the calyx with Clover. Shade on the dark side with a little Green Dark. Highlight with Warm White.
8. Shade the stem with Green Dark. Highlight with Warm White.

Curlicues:

Using the #3 round watercolor brush filled with thinned Green Umber, create the curlicues.

Flyspecking:

Using an old toothbrush filled with thinned Red Light, Green Umber, and just a little Warm White, do the flyspecking. Let dry thoroughly.

FINISHING

1. Varnish the painting with several coats of waterbase varnish. Let dry thoroughly.
2. Attach coat hooks, following package instructions. ❏

Painting a Sunflower

*Depth and variation are achieved by using three paint colors on the petals. Before the petals are painted, they are under-coated with several coats of Pure Gold. Let the paint dry between each coat, and let cure. Then the petals are stroked with Lemon Custard. Several coats will be needed to cover. Let dry. Then you're ready to add the final petal colors and paint the center. Use a large flat brush for the petals. The photos show the final colors being added **without the undercoating** so that you can see better the strokes that are being made.*

Paint the petals:

1. To paint the petals using the final petal colors, paint each half of a petal with an "S" stroke. This shows Turner's Yellow used to paint half of the petal.

2. Paint the other half of the petal with an "S" stroke.

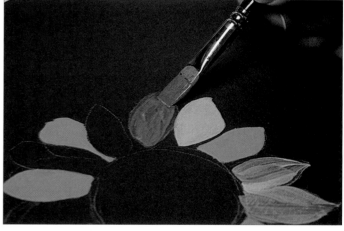

3. Paint some of the petals with Yellow Ochre.

4. Paint some of the petals with Medium Yellow.

5. Add blending medium on top of painted petals before shading.

Shade around the center:

6. Use a flat brush sideloaded with floating medium and Burnt Sienna to float shading between petals for more definition.

7. Use the same sideloaded flat brush to float shading on each petal around the center. An option for this is to use an old scruffy brush (such as an old stencil brush), dab a little Burnt Sienna around the center and slightly on the petals. Wipe the brush on a rag. Pick up a little bit of Red Light. Dab Red Light over the Burnt Sienna.

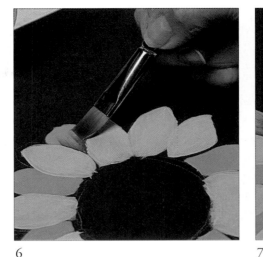

6

7

8. Clean up the tips of the petals and add highlighting by applying Medium Yellow.

Paint the center:

9. Using the stencil brush, dab Burnt Umber in the center to stipple.

10. To highlight the center, dab on Red Light.

11. On the same brush, pick up Medium Yellow, Yellow Ochre, and Pure Orange to complete the highlighting.

Sunflower Worksheet

Fig. 1
Undercoat with Pure Gold. Let dry. Paint petals with Lemon Custard.

Fig. 3
Dab paint on the center.

Red Light

Burnt Umber

Fig. 2
Paint the petals with three colors. Shade around the center.

Turner's Yellow

Burnt Sienna

Medium Yellow

Yellow Ochre

Fig. 4
Highlight the center.

Medium Yellow

Yellow Ochre

Red Light

Pure Orange

Sunflower Bud Worksheet

Lemon Custard

Pure Gold

Fig. 1
Undercoat with Pure Gold. Let dry.
Paint petals with Lemon Custard.

Yellow Ochre

Medium Yellow

Turner's Yellow

Burnt Sienna

Warm White

Hauser Greer Dark

Clover undercoat

Fig. 2
Paint petals with three colors. Shade
around calyx with Burnt Sienna.
Undercoat calyx and stem with Clover.
Shade "petals" of calyx with Green
Dark. Highlight with Warm White.

Fig. 3
Add Red Light on top of Burnt Sienna
shading. Shade stem with Green Dark.
Highlight with Warm White.

Warm White

Hauser
Green Dark

Sunflower Pattern
Enlarge @200%

Section A

Join section A to section B
at dotted lines

A   A

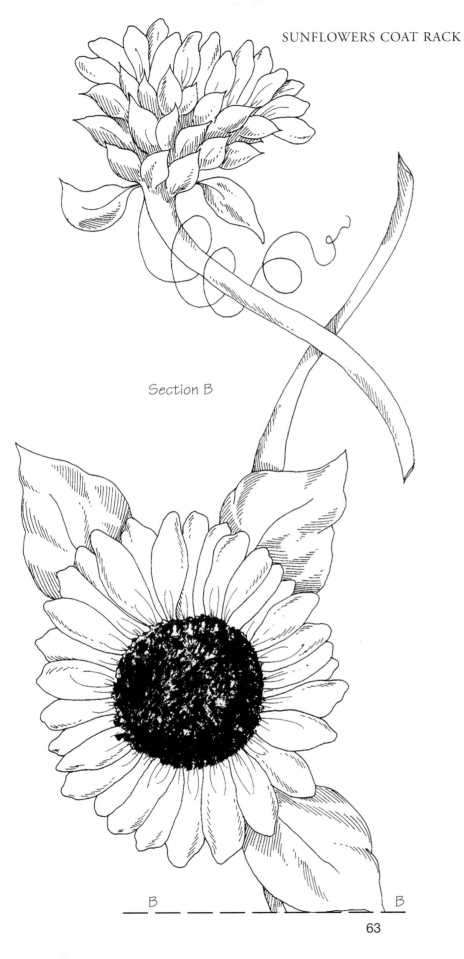

Section B

B — — — — — — — — B

Painting a Quick & Easy Leaf

This leaf works nicely for many of the projects in this book. It is the leaf used for the lilacs, sunflowers, and lemons. The Leaf Worksheet illustrates the technique, step by step.

PALETTE OF COLORS

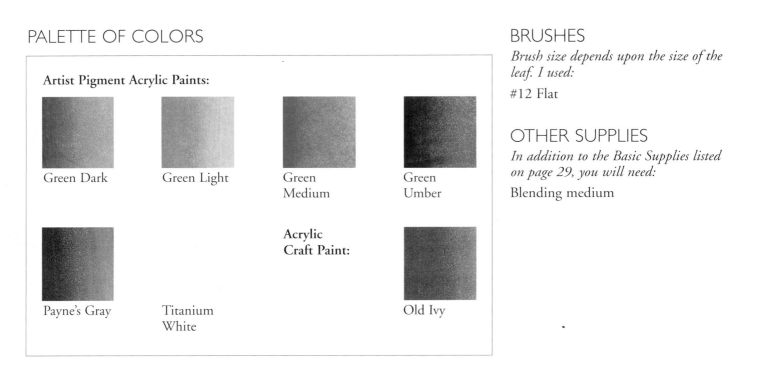

Artist Pigment Acrylic Paints:

Green Dark   Green Light   Green Medium   Green Umber

Acrylic Craft Paint:

Payne's Gray   Titanium White   Old Ivy

BRUSHES

Brush size depends upon the size of the leaf. I used:

#12 Flat

OTHER SUPPLIES

In addition to the Basic Supplies listed on page 29, you will need:

Blending medium

INSTRUCTIONS

Refer to the Leaf Worksheet, opposite.

1. Undercoat the leaf with Old Ivy. (Fig. 1) Two or three coats will be needed to cover. Let dry and cure.
2. Double-load your brush with water and Green Umber (or a shadow color of your choice). Blend on the palette so the color blends through the brush from dark to medium to light. Float the shadow color at the base and shadow areas of the leaf. (Fig. 2) Let dry and cure.
3. Apply a small amount of blending medium over the leaf. (Fig. 3)
4. Wipe the brush. Add Green Umber, Green Dark, Green Medium, and Titanium White. (Fig. 4)
5. Wipe the brush. Using a very light touch, blend from the base of the leaf out toward the edges. (Fig. 5) Lift the brush as you pull toward the edges, letting it take off like an airplane lifting off the runway. You don't want to pull the color out over the edges. If needed, apply more blending medium and paint.
6. Lightly blend from the outside edges back toward the base, merging the colors lightly together, following the shape of the leaf. (Fig. 6) If you want a darker leaf, use more of the shadow color or Green Dark. For a lighter leaf, use more Green Light and Titanium White. ❑

Leaf Worksheet

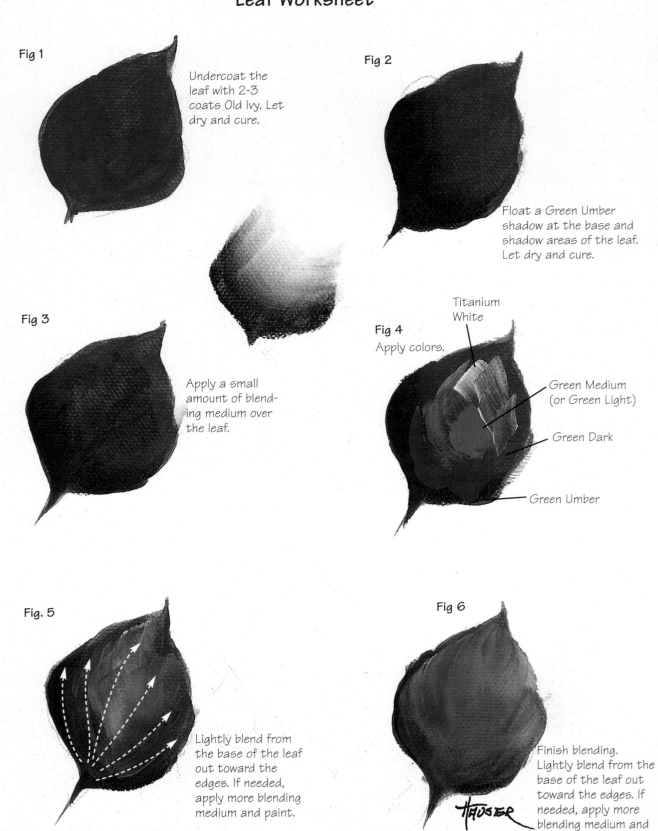

Fig 1

Undercoat the leaf with 2-3 coats Old Ivy. Let dry and cure.

Fig 2

Float a Green Umber shadow at the base and shadow areas of the leaf. Let dry and cure.

Fig 3

Apply a small amount of blending medium over the leaf.

Fig 4
Apply colors.

Titanium White

Green Medium (or Green Light)

Green Dark

Green Umber

Fig. 5

Lightly blend from the base of the leaf out toward the edges. If needed, apply more blending medium and paint.

Fig 6

Finish blending. Lightly blend from the base of the leaf out toward the edges. If needed, apply more blending medium and paint.

HAUSER

Leaf Bordered Picture Frame

I call these very simple leaves "gel leaves" because they are painted with a gel-like blending medium and just a touch of color. Flowing lines are then added with a liner brush full of paint with an ink-like consistency.
I've put these leaves on an old wooden frame. The effect is elegant, yet they are so quick and easy to do.

PALETTE OF COLORS

Artist Pigment Acrylic Paints:	Acrylic Craft Paint:
Green	Winter
Umber	White

SURFACE
Wooden picture frame for 5" x 7" photo

PREPARATION
1. Clean the frame and sand, if needed, with fine sandpaper.
2. Wipe with a tack cloth.
3. Apply two or more coats Winter White. Allow the paint to dry between each coat. Let dry and cure.
4. Sand off the paint on some edges to create a distressed look.
5. Neatly trace and transfer the design using colored chalk or your preferred method.

PAINTING THE DESIGN
See the Leaf Border Worksheet.
1. Anchor a shadow of Green Umber at the base of each leaf. To do this, double-load the brush with water and Green Umber. Blend on the palette and float on the anchor. Let dry and cure.

BRUSHES
The size of brush depends upon the size of leaf. I used:
#10 Flat
#1 Liner
Sponge brush for painting surface

OTHER SUPPLIES
In addition to the Basic Supplies listed on page 29, you will need:
Blending medium
Satin waterbase varnish

2. Apply a small amount of blending medium to the leaf.
3. Reapply a little Green Umber on top of the shadowed area. Using a light touch, carefully blend the Green Umber into the blending medium.
4. Thin Green Umber with water until the paint is the consistency of ink and carefully fill a #1 liner brush. Apply small groups of berries (small dots grouped together here and there) as desired.
5. Paint many fine lines intertwining and connecting the leaves.
6. Outline the leaves, if desired. Let the painting dry and cure.

FINISHING
1. Varnish with two or more coats of satin water-based varnish. Let dry.
2. Rub with a piece of brown paper bag with no printing on it to smooth the surface. ❏

''With brush in hand
my mind empties of its
sorrows and the beauty
in this life smiles.''

Priscilla Hauser

Leaf Border Worksheet

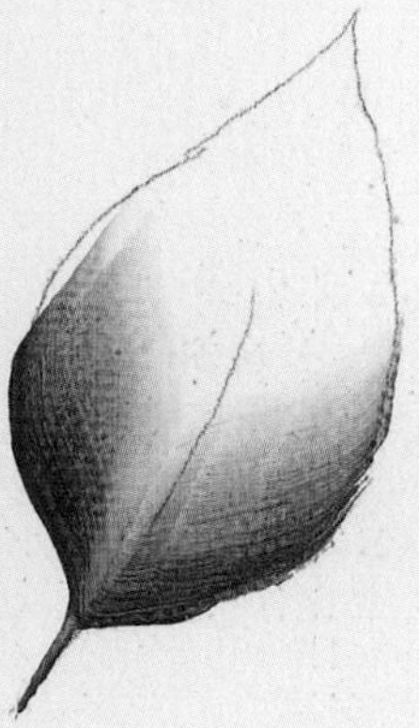

Fig. 1
Anchor with
Green Umber.

Fig. 2
Apply blending
medium.

Fig. 3
Blend Green
Umber into
blending medium.

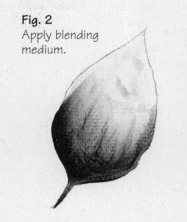

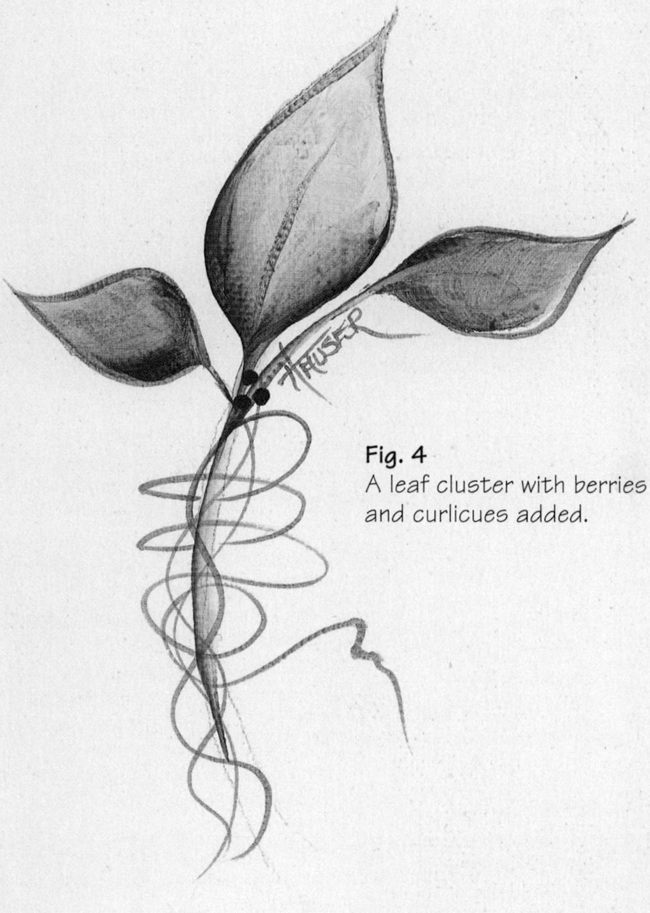

Fig. 4
A leaf cluster with berries
and curlicues added.

Pattern for
Leaf Bordered Picture Frame
Actual Size

Blueberries Ensemble

These three pieces (a table, a folding chair, and a lamp) were designed to coordinate with each other. They were very quick and easy to do — the leaves were stamped with pre-cut foam stamps and the berries were created with a round sponge brush. Practice the stamping and sponging first on a brown paper bag or other piece of paper. You'll be fascinated with the results you achieve. Although you can be as elaborate as you like with floats when shading, simplicity is often the best. It can be just as charming, if not more so, than elaborate shading.

This is a perfect opportunity to try painting the design freehand because you will be using leaf stamps and a round sponge brush to accomplish the undercoating. If you wish to try freehanding on a large surface such as a table, create three groups of leaves and berries. Make one group large-sized, one medium-sized, and one small-sized. Connect the groups with vines to which you add a few leaves. If you prefer, you can, of course, trace and transfer the design using gray graphite.

Instructions begin on page 72.
Lamp is pictured on page 73.

70

PALETTE OF COLORS

Artist Pigment Acrylic Paints:

Burnt Umber

Green Dark

Green Umber

Ice Green Light

Prussian Blue

Titanium White

True Burgundy

Acrylic Craft Paints:

Fresh Foliage

Thunder Blue

True Blue

BRUSHES

Flats - #4, #8, #12

Liners - #1, #2

1" flat synthetic (for floating background color and varnishing)

Round sponge brush, 1/4" (for stamping the berries)

SURFACES

Wood folding chair

Wooden side table, flea market find

White ceramic lamp base

OTHER SUPPLIES

In addition to the Basic Supplies listed on page 29, you will need:

Medium size sea sponge

Blue painter's masking tape

Floating medium

Waterbase varnish

Matte sealer spray

Leaf-shaped foam stamps, 1" and 3/4" long

Latex wall paint in eggshell finish for painting furniture: ivory white

Sea sponge

PREPARATION

Table & Chair:

The table and chair were purchased with a distressed white finish. Here's how to duplicate the look:

1. Sand the surface with fine grade sandpaper. Wipe with a tack cloth.
2. Apply two coats of ivory white latex wall paint, using a 1" flat synthetic brush or a sponge brush. Allow the paint to dry between coats.
3. Sand with fine grade sandpaper on the edges to give a worn look.

Ceramic Lamp Base:

1. Spray with matte sealer to give the slick surface a little "tooth." Let dry.

2. Transfer the design. *Option:* Paint freehand.

APPLYING THE BACKGROUND COLOR

See the Blueberries Worksheet.

Table:

1. Draw a line on the table top approximately 2" from the table edge. Apply painter's masking tape along the inside of the line, placing the straight edge of the tape facing the table edge to create a border. (When you place the pattern on the surface, or freehand the design, this line will be the outside edge for the placement of the leaves and berries. You will conceal it with the connecting vines and stems.)

Continued on page 74

73

Continued from page 72

2. Using the sea sponge, dampen the border area with clean water.

3. Thin Thunder Blue to an ink-like consistency on the palette and sponge it on the wet border, working from the tape edge to the table edge. Keep it light and airy, and develop it from dark to medium to light as you move away from the tape. If it becomes too dark, use a damp rag to wipe it back.

4. While still wet, remove the tape and soften the painted edge along the tape line, using a damp rag.

Chair & Lamp:

1. Using the sponge, dampen the design area with clean water.

2. Thin Thunder Blue to an ink-like consistency on the palette and sponge it on the design area. Keep it light and airy. Let dry completely.

PAINTING THE DESIGN

See the Blueberries Worksheet.

Leaves:

1. Working one leaf at a time, apply a coat of Fresh Foliage to the surface of the stamp using a #8 flat brush. Stamp one or two leaves at a time on the surface. (This undercoat will be somewhat transparent and may appear messy at this point – that's okay.)

2. Adjust the shapes of the leaves by painting with Fresh Foliage where necessary. Let dry.

3. Using a #12 flat brush, shade the base of each leaf with a Green Umber float.

4. Shade the left side and the tip of each leaf with a Green Umber float.

5. Accent each leaf with either a True Burgundy float or a Green Dark float.

6. Highlight the right side of each leaf with an Ice Green float.

Blueberries:

1. Load the 1/4" round sponge brush with True Blue. To stamp the berries, press it on the surface and slightly twist as you lift it. Allow this undercoat to dry completely.

2. Make an ice blue mix (Titanium White + tiny touch Prussian Blue + tiny touch Burnt Umber). Pick up Thunder Blue on one side of the round sponge brush and the ice blue mix on the other side. Dab on the palette (turning the sponge brush slightly as you dab) to blend the colors.

3. Twist the sponge brush as you apply it to the surface on top of the dry True Blue undercoat. Let dry.
4. Accent some of the berries with a True Burgundy float.
5. Use the liner brush filled with thinned Thunder Blue to paint a star on the blossom end of some berries. Let dry.
6. Using a #4 flat brush, highlight around the stars with a float of the ice blue mix.
7. On other berries, paint an "upside-down crown" on the blossom end, using a liner brush filled with thinned Thunder Blue.

Vines & Stems:
1. Using the tip of the #2 liner brush, undercoat the stems with Fresh Foliage.
2. Using a #4 flat brush, shade the stems along the bottom with an Green Umber float.
3. Shade the stems where they go behind leaves or other stems with a Green Umber float.
4. Accent some of the shaded areas with a True Burgundy float.
5. Highlight along the top with an Ice Green float.

FINISHING

Table:
1. Add curlicues to the design using a liner brush and thinned Green Umber. Allow to dry completely.
2. On the table, add floats of Thunder Blue to the inside edge of the design and throughout the design, using a #12 flat brush.
3. Paint edge of table and decorate edge with Thunder Blue. Allow to dry completely.
4. Apply two coats of waterbase varnish.

Chair:
1. Add curlicues to the design using a liner brush and thinned Green Umber. Allow to dry completely.
2. Apply two coats of waterbase varnish.

Lamp:
1. Add curlicues to the design using a liner brush and thinned Green Umber. Allow to dry completely.
2. Paint the base of the lamp with Thunder Blue.
3. Mist with spray sealer. Let dry. ❑

Blueberries Worksheet

Background:

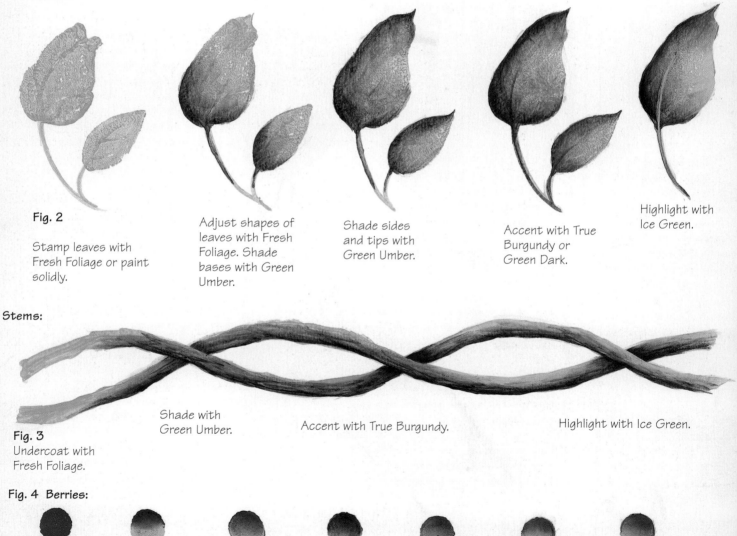

Fig. 1

On the table, draw a line 2" from outside edge of table. Place tape along line.

Wet surface. Sponge on thinned Thunder Blue.

Leaves:

Fig. 2

Stamp leaves with Fresh Foliage or paint solidly.

Adjust shapes of leaves with Fresh Foliage. Shade bases with Green Umber.

Shade sides and tips with Green Umber.

Accent with True Burgundy or Green Dark.

Highlight with Ice Green.

Stems:

Shade with Green Umber.

Accent with True Burgundy.

Highlight with Ice Green.

Fig. 3
Undercoat with Fresh Foliage.

Fig. 4 Berries:

Dab Thunder Blue undercoat.

Dab with Thunder Blue and Ice Blue mix.

Twist as you lift.

Accent some with True Burgundy.

Paint the blossom end "star" with Thunder Blue.

Add a float with the ice blue mix.

A berry with a Thunder Blue "upside down crown."

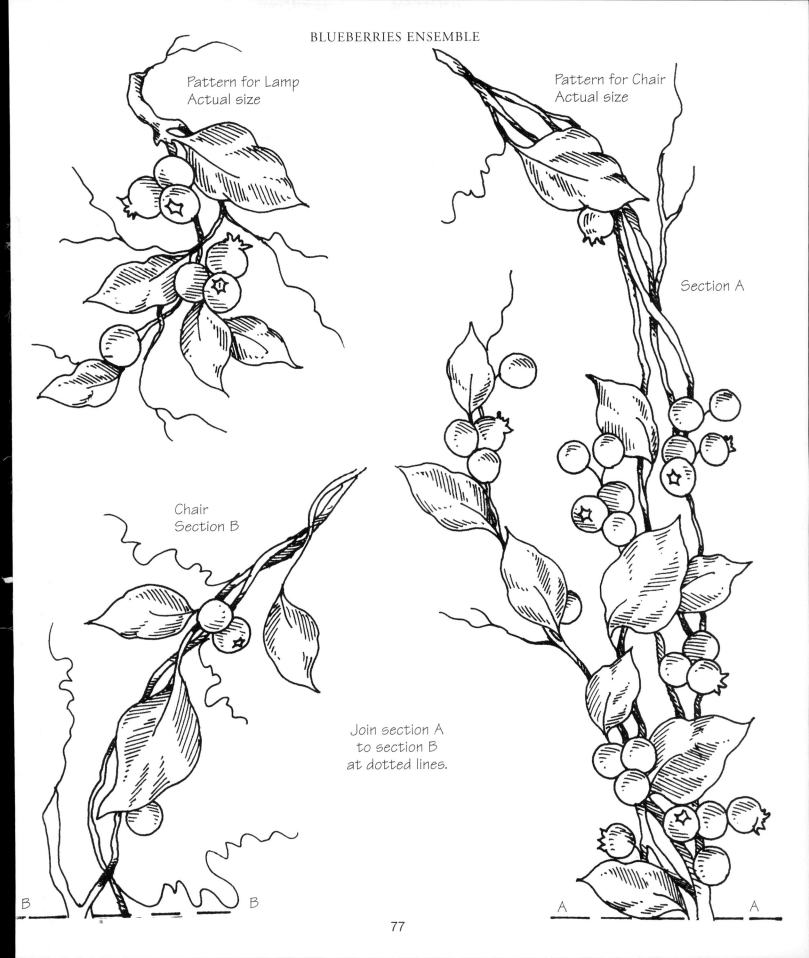

Pattern for Lamp
Actual size

Pattern for Chair
Actual size

Section A

Chair
Section B

Join section A
to section B
at dotted lines.

B   B

A   A

Pattern for Table
Enlarge @200%

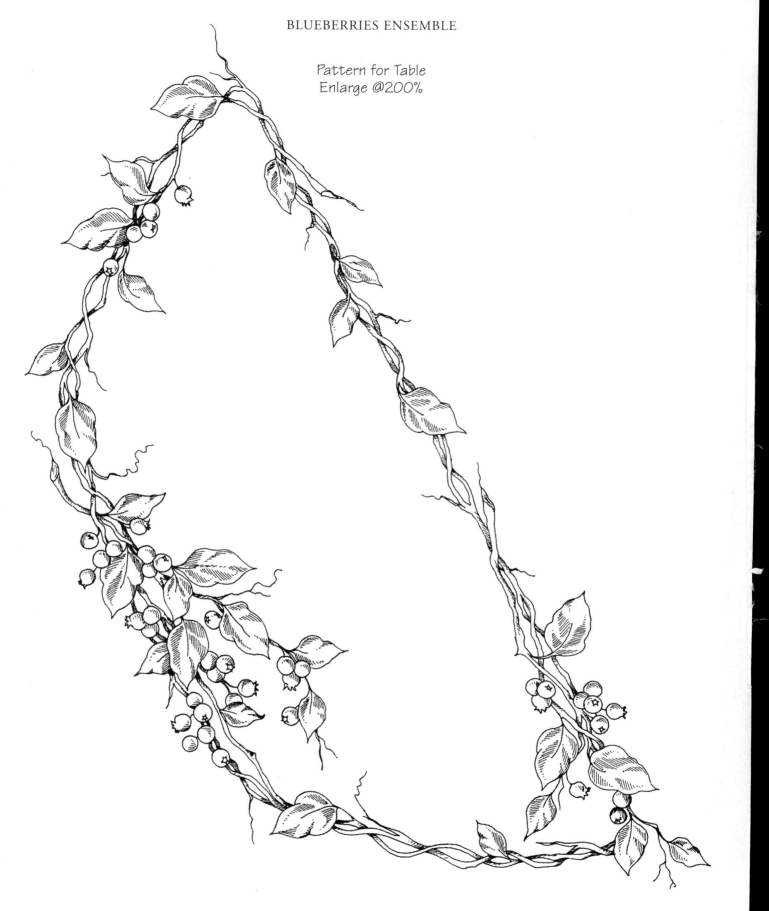

Pictured above: Blueberries Chair, closeup.

Garden Window

PALETTE OF COLORS

**Oils or
Artist Pigment Acrylic Paints:**

Bright
Green

Burnt
Sienna

Burnt
Umber

Cadmium
Orange

Cadmium
Yellow
Medium

Cerulean
Blue

Phthalo Red
Rose

Phthalo
Yellow
Green

Titanium
White

Viridian

I liked the paint color of this wonderful, old leaded glass window so much that I didn't do anything to the frame but clean it. You could paint this design on any old window or a large frame.

To paint on the glass, I used oil paints. However, this project could be done with acrylics as well. Instructions for using both types of paint are included. If you want to use acrylics, you will need to neatly undercoat the designs on the glass with a glass and tile medium. Allow the medium to dry and cure for two weeks before beginning the painting. (When using oil paints, this step is not necessary.)

Applying gold leaf to the backs of the flowers and pots painted on the glass will make the painted designs opaque, so no light will pass through them. This opacity is desirable if you wish to hang the window where light will pass through the glass from behind. The gold leaf also produces a nicer-looking finish on the back of the window. If desired, you could paint the design over the gold leaf on the back of the window so the painting will be on both sides of the window.

BRUSHES

Flats - #4, #8, #10, #12
Liner - #1

SURFACE

Old window, flea market find

OTHER SUPPLIES

In addition to the Basic Supplies listed on page 29, you will need:
Scissors
Double-sided tape
Rubbing alcohol
Waterbase varnish, satin sheen

If using oil paints on the glass:
Disposable paper palette pad (to use as a palette for oil paint)
Odorless turpentine
Baby oil
Wax paper

If using acrylic paints on the glass:
Glass and tile medium
Blending medium

For gold leafing:
Gold leaf
Gold leaf sizing
An old paint brush (for applying leaf)
Piece of velveteen (to burnish the gold leaf)

Instructions begin on page 82.

PREPARATION

1. Sand the frame of the window with fine grade sandpaper to remove any cracking or flaking paint.
2. Wipe with a tack cloth.
3. Carefully and thoroughly clean the glass panes on both sides with alcohol. Let dry.
4. Trace the pots of flowers on tracing paper.
5. Apply double-stick tape to the tracing paper in two places. Stick the pattern to the back of the glass.

PAINTING THE DESIGN

See the Garden Window Worksheet.
Pots:
If using oil paints, thin the paint with odorless turpentine to the consistency of creamy icing. A benefit of using oils is you can easily wipe them off and start over.
1. Mix Burnt Sienna + Titanium White (1:4). Apply the paint colors as shown on the worksheet.
2. Wipe the brush and blend, using a light touch.

PAINTING THE LEAVES:

The Garden Window Worksheet shows three color combinations for leaves.
First Leaf:
1. Using a light touch, undercoat with Bright Green. Let dry, if desired.
2. Apply more Bright Green. Shade the base with Viridian.
3. Wipe the brush. Gently blend the edge of Viridian into the edge of Bright Green.

Second Leaf:
1. Undercoat with Bright Green.
2. Shade dark with Viridian.
3. Highlight with Phthalo Yellow Green.

Third Leaf:
1. Undercoat with Bright Green.
2. Shade with Viridian.

TIPS FOR PAINTING WITH OILS

- Clean off any paint that gets on your skin with baby oil.

- Keep odorless turpentine in a glass jar with a tight lid. Keep the lid on the jar unless you are using the turpentine in a way that won't release excess fumes into the room.

- Always work in a well-ventilated area.

- Use a good, flexible, straight-blade palette knife when mixing odorless turpentine into oil colors to create the proper consistency.

- For the flowers and leaves, the paint should be the consistency of very soft spreadable butter or cake icing.

- For line work, the paint should be the consistency of ink.

- Always use a light touch when blending.

3. Highlight with a mixture of Titanium White + Viridian (4:1).

PAINTING THE FLOWERS

See the Garden Window Worksheet.
Pink Flower:
1. Paint the petals with a mixture of Phthalo Red Rose + Titanium White (1:4).
2. Wipe the brush. Apply a rim of Phthalo Red Rose around the outside edge of each petal.
3. Wipe the brush. Use a light touch to blend the edges of the colors where they meet.
4. Paint the center with Cadmium Yellow Light.
5. Fill a #1 liner brush with Phthalo Red Rose that has been thinned to an ink-like consistency with odorless turpentine. Paint swirls into the wet yellow.

Yellow Flower:
1. Paint the petals with Cadmium Yellow Medium.
2. Apply Cadmium Orange around the outside edge of each petal.
3. Wipe the brush. Blend where the orange meets the yellow.
4. Paint the center with Cadmium Orange. Shade with Burnt Sienna.
5. Thin Burnt Sienna with odorless turpentine to an

ink-like consistency. Use the point of the liner brush to apply the dots to the center.

Blue Flower:

1. Apply Cerulean Blue at the center of each petal.
2. Mix Cerulean Blue + Titanium White (1:4). Paint the outer petals with this color.
3. Wipe the brush. Blend where the colors meet.
4. Paint the center with Titanium White. Let dry.
5. Using a liner brush with thinned Burnt Sienna, paint the cross-hatching in the center of the flower.
6. Thin Titanium White to an ink-like consistency. Apply dots around the center.

Stems:

1. Paint with Bright Green.
2. Shade with Viridian. Let the paint dry and cure completely.

Acrylic Option

If using acrylics, follow these steps. If the acrylics lift, it is because the undercoats have not cured long enough:

1. Apply glass and tile medium to the design area. Let dry and cure for 10 days.
2. Apply a small amount of blending medium to each area of the design. Complete one area at a time.
3. Apply the colors as shown on the worksheet.
4. Wipe the brush and blend, using a light touch.
5. Paint only one small area at a time because acrylics dry quickly.

TIPS FOR DRYING OIL PAINTS

- Remember oil paints take a long time to dry and cure. It even takes longer when you paint with oils on glass because the glass is not porous – curing could take as long as two weeks.

- To accelerate drying, place the window in a room that is 72 degrees F. or warmer. Have a fan in the room gently blowing in the direction of the painting.

- Low humidity helps accelerate drying time. ❑

PAINTING THE LETTERING & FINISHING THE FRAME

1. Neatly transfer the lettering to the window frame.
2. Fill a good flat brush full of thinned Titanium White acrylic paint.
3. Neatly paint the letters. I left them a bit transparent and did not apply a second coat. If a more opaque look is desired, go over the letters a second time. Let dry.
4. Apply two or more coats of satin varnish to the frame.

APPLYING THE GOLD LEAFING

The photos that follow show the leafing process.

1. Using an old brush, neatly apply gold leaf sizing to the back sides of the flower, leaves, and pots. Use only a small amount, and spread it out. Apply the sizing carefully so it only covers the painted design.
2. When the milkiness of the sizing subsides, apply a sheet of leafing. To handle the leaf, first cut it into squares of needed sizes. Place a sheet of wax paper over the leafing. Rub your hands together, and place your hand on the waxed paper. The heat from your hand will cause the leafing to adhere to the wax paper.
3. Position the leafing over the sizing and press firmly with your hand. Remove the wax paper. Let sit for 24 hours.
4. Using a soft piece of velveteen, burnish (rub) the leafing to remove excess pieces. ❑

Applying Gold Leafing

These photos show a flower that is painted on a pane of glass.

1. Apply gold leaf sizing carefully to the design area on the back of the painted glass.

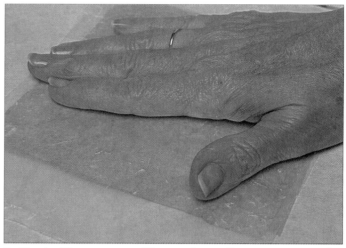

2. Cut leaf into squares. Place a sheet of wax paper over the leafing. Rub your hands together, and place you hand on the waxed paper. The heat from your hand will cause the leafing to adhere to the wax paper.

3. Position the leafing over the sizing on the glass and press firmly with your hand. Remove the wax paper. Let sit for 24 hours.

4. Using a soft piece of velveteen, burnish (rub) the leafing to remove excess pieces.

The finished leafing. See how it adheres only to the design area. ❏

Yellow Flower

Flower Patterns
Actual Size

Blue Flower

Yellow Flower

Garden Window Worksheet

Pot

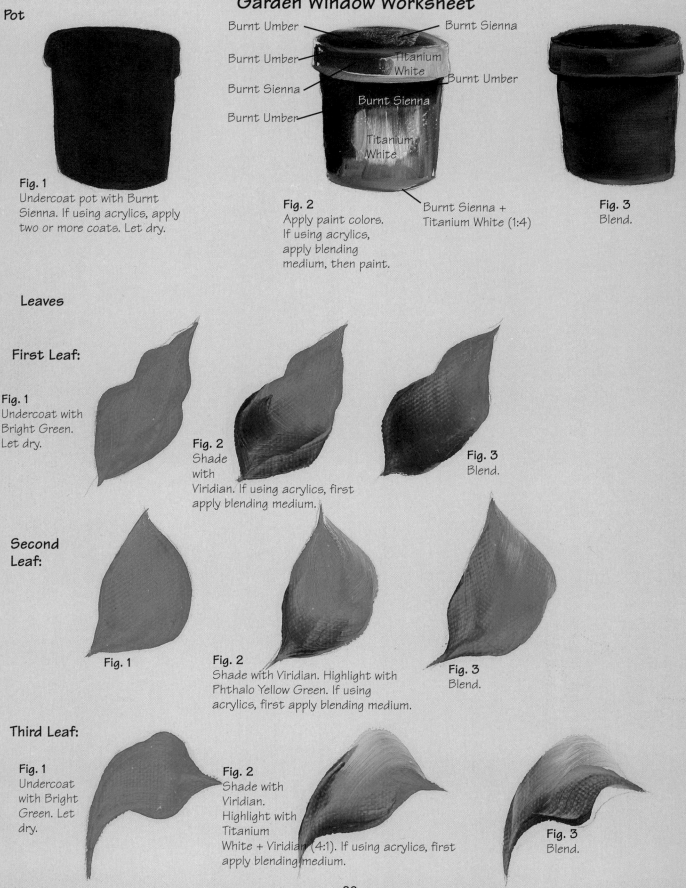

Fig. 1
Undercoat pot with Burnt Sienna. If using acrylics, apply two or more coats. Let dry.

Burnt Umber — — Burnt Sienna

Burnt Umber — — Titanium White

Burnt Sienna — — Burnt Umber

Burnt Umber — Burnt Sienna

Titanium White

Fig. 2
Apply paint colors. If using acrylics, apply blending medium, then paint.

Burnt Sienna + Titanium White (1:4)

Fig. 3
Blend.

Leaves

First Leaf:

Fig. 1
Undercoat with Bright Green. Let dry.

Fig. 2
Shade with Viridian. If using acrylics, first apply blending medium.

Fig. 3
Blend.

Second Leaf:

Fig. 1

Fig. 2
Shade with Viridian. Highlight with Phthalo Yellow Green. If using acrylics, first apply blending medium.

Fig. 3
Blend.

Third Leaf:

Fig. 1
Undercoat with Bright Green. Let dry.

Fig. 2
Shade with Viridian. Highlight with Titanium White + Viridian (4:1). If using acrylics, first apply blending medium.

Fig. 3
Blend.

86

Garden Window Worksheet

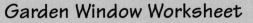

Pink Flower

Fig. 1
Paint petals with Phthalo Red Rose + Titanium White (1:4).

Fig. 2
Shade with Phthalo Red Rose.

Fig. 3
Blend. Paint center with Cadmium Yellow Light. Add line work with Phthalo Red Rose.

Yellow Flower

Fig. 1
Paint petals with Cadmium Yellow Medium.

Fig. 2
Apply Cadmium Orange around the outside of each petal.

Fig. 3
Blend. Paint center with Cadmium Orange. Shade with Burnt Sienna. Add dots with Burnt Sienna.

Blue Flower

Fig. 1
Apply Cerulean Blue at the center at each petal.

Fig. 2
Mix Cerulean Blue + Titanium White (1:4). Paint outer petals.

Fig. 3
Blend. Paint Burnt Sienna on the center. Add dots with Titanium White.

Hauser

Lettering Pattern
Actual Size

There's no
place I'd
rather be

than in my garden

Pink Flower Pattern
Actual Size

Ladybug Garden Set

Ladybug, ladybug - come paint with me.
We'll paint a wagon and flower pots, you'll see.
Garden accessories for one and all,
How beautifully you'll adorn them, large and small.
We'll paint your portrait one day very soon,
All done, all done on a Sunday afternoon.

*This wonderful little old wagon cleaned up quickly
and easily. I think it would make a neat centerpiece for
a garden party – can't you just see it filled with cute
shower gifts? In addition to a wagon, I've painted
coordinating flower pots, garden gloves, and a
cultivating fork.*

*And yes, it can all be created in an afternoon. Just
follow the easy instructions and step-by-step worksheets,
adding your own touches. Most of all, have fun!*

Instructions follow on page 92

PALETTE OF COLORS

Artist Pigment Acrylic Paints:

Burnt Umber	Naphthol Crimson	Payne's Gray	Prussian Blue

Pure Black	Pure Orange	Titanium White	True Burgundy

Turner's Yellow	Ice Blue Mix

Acrylic Craft Paints:

Licorice	Lipstick Red	Whipped Berry	Wicker White

BRUSHES

#20 Flat

#1 Liner

Old toothbrush (for flyspecking)

Round sponge brushes, 1-3/4", 5/8", 1/4"

Sponge brush for painting surface

SURFACES

Small wood wagon, approx. 6" wide x 12" long

4" clay pots

Garden tools and gloves

OTHER SUPPLIES

In addition to the Basic Supplies listed on page 29, you will need:

Glazing medium

Textile medium

Painter's masking tape

Dish detergent

Waterbase varnish, matte or satin sheen

PREPARATION

Wagon & Flower Pots:
1. Wash the piece, if needed, with a mild detergent. Rinse and wipe dry.
2. Sand the surface, if needed. Wipe with a tack cloth.
3. Paint the wagon Wicker White. Let dry.
4. Neatly trace and transfer the design to the surfaces using gray graphite or chalk.

Garden Gloves:
1. Wash with mild detergent.
2. Let dry thoroughly.
3. Transfer the design to the gloves with chalk.

Cultivating Fork:
1. Sand the handle slightly.
2. Wipe with a tack cloth.
3. Paint the handle Wicker White. Let dry.
4. Transfer the design.

PAINTING THE LARGE LADYBUGS

The large ladybugs are painted on the wagon. See the Ladybug Worksheet.

Ladybug Heads & Legs:
1. Dip the 5/8" round sponge brush in Pure Black. Blot on a damp paper towel or rag several times to remove excess paint.

2. Press the sponge brush on the surface and wiggle it gently from side to side. Repeat this three times (as shown on the Ladybug Worksheet) to form the head.

3. Thin Pure Black with water to an ink-like consistency. Fill the liner brush with the thinned paint and neatly paint the legs and antennae. Let dry.

4. Make an ice blue mix with Titanium White + a tiny touch of Prussian Blue + a tiny touch Burnt Umber. Paint the detail work on the head and neck, using a liner brush filled with the thinned ice blue mix.

Ladybug Bodies:

TIP: Practice using the 1-3/4" round sponge brush on a piece of paper a few times before painting your project.

1. Dip the 1-3/4" round sponge brush in Naphthol Crimson several times to be sure it is full of paint. Blot on a paper towel or rag to remove excess paint.

2. Press the sponge brush on the surface to form the body. Let dry.

3. Apply a little glazing medium. Double-load a large flat brush with glazing medium and Pure Orange. Float Pure Orange on the left side of the body.

4. Using the large flat brush, float True Burgundy on the lower right side of the body. Let dry.

5. Using the large flat brush with glazing medium, apply a highlight of Turner's Yellow on the upper left section of the body. Let dry.

Body Details:

1. Dip the 5/8" round sponge brush in Pure Black and blot. Press dots on the back of the ladybug.

2. For the smaller dots, use the 1/4" round sponge brush with Pure Black.

3. Fill the liner brush with thinned Pure Black and paint a line down the center of the ladybug's back. Let dry.

4. Fill the liner brush with thinned Turner's Yellow. Outline the edges of the black line. Let dry.

Shadow:

1. Using your large flat brush, apply a little glazing medium on the right side of the bug.

2. Pick up a tiny bit of Payne's Gray on the corner of your brush. Blend on your palette so the color graduates through your brush from dark to medium to light.

3. Paint Payne's Gray next to the body to form the shadow, letting it blend out into the glazing medium.

PAINTING THE TINY LADYBUGS

The tiny ladybugs are painted on the gloves and cultivating fork. See the Ladybug Worksheet; they are quick and easy. When painting on the gloves, mix equal amounts of textile medium and paint so the paints will be permanent when dry.

1. Using the #1 liner brush, paint the black areas.

2. Dip the 5/8" round sponge brush in Naphthol Crimson, blot on a rag, and paint a dot over the body area. Let dry.

3. Apply a little Pure Orange on the left side and a little True Burgundy on the right side.

4. Using a stylus or your liner brush with thinned Pure Black, paint the dots on the back.

PAINTING THE POTS

1. Seal the pots with a coat of waterbase varnish.

2. Let dry. Sand lightly.

3. Paint the pots with two or more coats Wicker White. Let the paint dry between each coat.

4. Use painter's tape to mask off stripes as shown in the photo.

5. Paint the stripes with Whipped Berry. Let dry.

6. Carefully remove the tape to expose the stripes.

FINISHING

Tip: Practice flyspecking on a blank piece of paper before specking the wagon or the cultivating fork.

Wagon:

1. Paint the inside of the wagon with two or more coats of Lipstick Red. Paint the wheels with Lipstick Red.

2. Trim the wheels with Licorice.

3. Using a toothbrush full of thinned Licorice, flyspeck the wagon. Let dry.

4. Apply several coats of waterbase varnish. Let dry between coats. Use a piece of brown paper bag with no printing on it to sand or rub between each dried coat of varnish. Let dry thoroughly.

Cultivating Fork:

1. Flyspeck, using thinned Licorice and the old toothbrush. Let dry.

2. Apply several coats of waterbase varnish. Let dry between coats.

Pots:

Varnish with two or more coats of waterbase varnish. ❏

Ladybug Worksheet

Large Ladybug

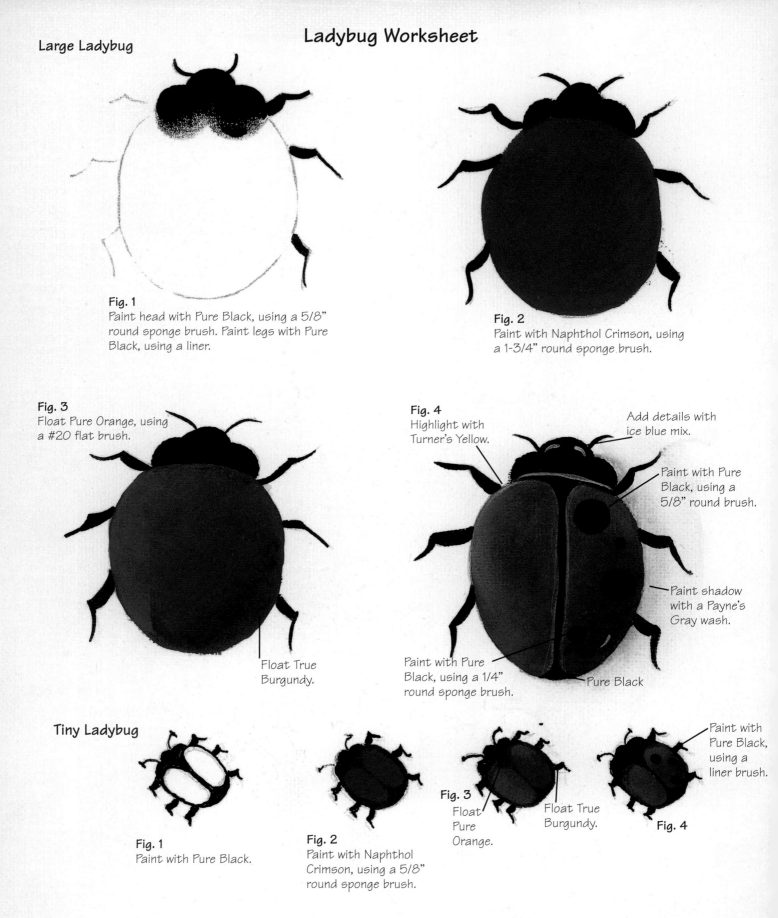

Fig. 1
Paint head with Pure Black, using a 5/8"
round sponge brush. Paint legs with Pure
Black, using a liner.

Fig. 2
Paint with Naphthol Crimson, using
a 1-3/4" round sponge brush.

Fig. 3
Float Pure Orange, using
a #20 flat brush.

Float True
Burgundy.

Fig. 4
Highlight with
Turner's Yellow.

Add details with
ice blue mix.

Paint with Pure
Black, using a
5/8" round brush.

Paint shadow
with a Payne's
Gray wash.

Paint with Pure
Black, using a 1/4"
round sponge brush.

Pure Black

Tiny Ladybug

Fig. 1
Paint with Pure Black.

Fig. 2
Paint with Naphthol
Crimson, using a 5/8"
round sponge brush.

Fig. 3
Float
Pure
Orange.

Float True
Burgundy.

Paint with
Pure Black,
using a
liner brush.

Fig. 4

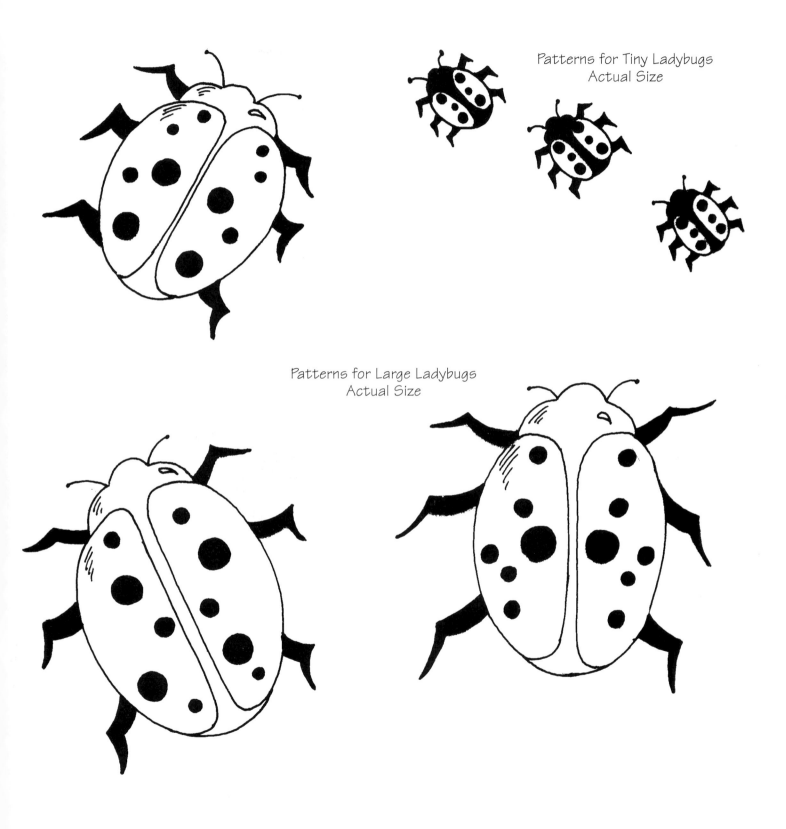

Patterns for Tiny Ladybugs
Actual Size

Patterns for Large Ladybugs
Actual Size

Seashells Headboard

When we found this old bed headboard, it was in terrible shape. We took it to a carpenter to have it restored, then painted it and added a design. This technique – pen and ink color wash – is fun and easy. I believe you'll have a lot of fun with it.

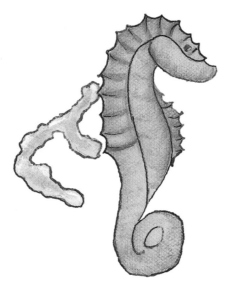

Instructions follow on page 98.

PALETTE OF COLORS

Artist Pigment Acrylic Paints:

Green
Umber

Titanium
White

Acrylic Craft Paints:

Barn Wood

Butter
Pecan

Clover

English
Mustard

Mint
Green

BRUSHES

Flats - #8, #14, #20

Liner - #1

Filbert - #4

Sponge brush, 2", for painting surface

Old toothbrush (for flyspecking)

SURFACE

Twin headboard, flea market find

OTHER SUPPLIES

In addition to the Basic Supplies listed on page 29, you will need:

Glazing medium

Quill pen and point #102 and brown waterproof ink *or* brown permanent ink marking pen

Waterbase varnish

Matte sealer spray

Latex wall paint in eggshell finish for painting bed, beige or parchment color

PREPARATION

1. Clean and repair the headboard, if needed.

2. Sand with fine grade sandpaper.

3. Wipe with a tack cloth.

4. Using a sponge brush, apply two or more coats of beige latex wall paint to cover. Allow the paint to dry between each coat.

5. Neatly trace and transfer the design, centering the design on the headboard. TIP: Often ink will bead up over graphite carbon lines, and chalk lines can clog a pen. I recommend turning the traced design over to the back side and going over the lines firmly with a #2 graphite pencil. (I know it's still graphite, but it won't be as greasy as graphite carbon paper.)

Continued on page 100

Pictured above: *Seashells Headboard, BEFORE.*

How to Ink & Shade Seashells

These photos show how to ink, apply washes, and shade the seashell design with floats of color.

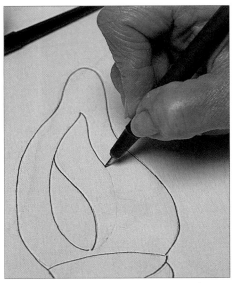

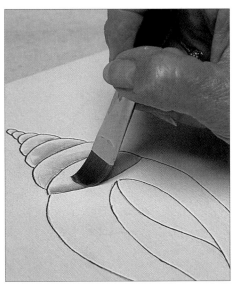

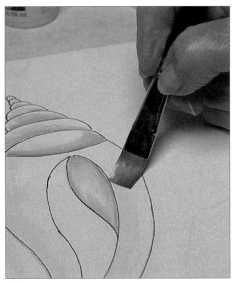

1. Ink over the transferred lines with permanent ink.

2. Wash color along inked lines (here, English Mustard).

3. Clean the brush. Apply a wash of the second color (here, Mint Green).

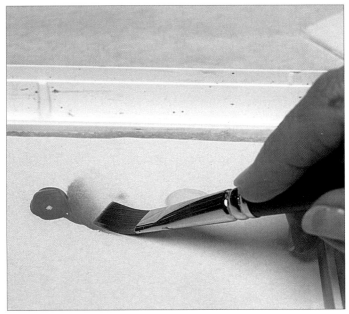

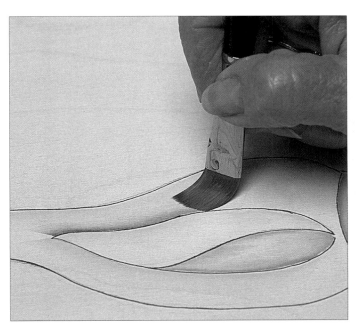

4. Clean the brush and load with glazing medium. Sideload with a shading color (here, English Mustard). Float shading along the inked lines to add dimension.

5. Load a brush with glazing medium. Sideload with paint and apply shading (here, Green Umber).

Continued from page 98

INKING THE DESIGN LINES

1. Carefully go over the design lines with brown ink. Embellish the pattern with coral and seaweed as desired, using the photo as a guide. TIP: There is no such thing as a mistake. If the pen slips, add a little more seaweed here and there – no one will ever know the difference.
2. Spray lightly with matte sealer to seal the ink. Let dry.

FLYSPECKING

See the Seaweed Worksheet.

Flyspeck the design area with Barn Wood, Mint Green, Butter Pecan, and a little Clover. Let dry and cure.

PAINTING THE DESIGN

The Seashells Worksheet includes the colors used for painting the elements of the design.

1. Make the washes. Rather than using water, which could cause the ink to run, use glazing medium. Mix a tiny touch of color into the glazing medium until the desired shade is achieved.
2. Paint the background seaweed, using the worksheet examples as guides.
3. Paint the coral, seaweed, and shells with the colors shown on the Seashells Worksheet.
4. Apply shading and highlights as shown on the Seashells Worksheet. Let dry.

INKING THE DETAILS

Use the pen to ink the details, adding as many as you desire. The more inking done, the prettier; the less inking, the faster you finish – it's up to you.

FINISHING

1. Lightly spray with matte sealer. Let dry completely.
2. Apply two or more coats of waterbase varnish. ❑

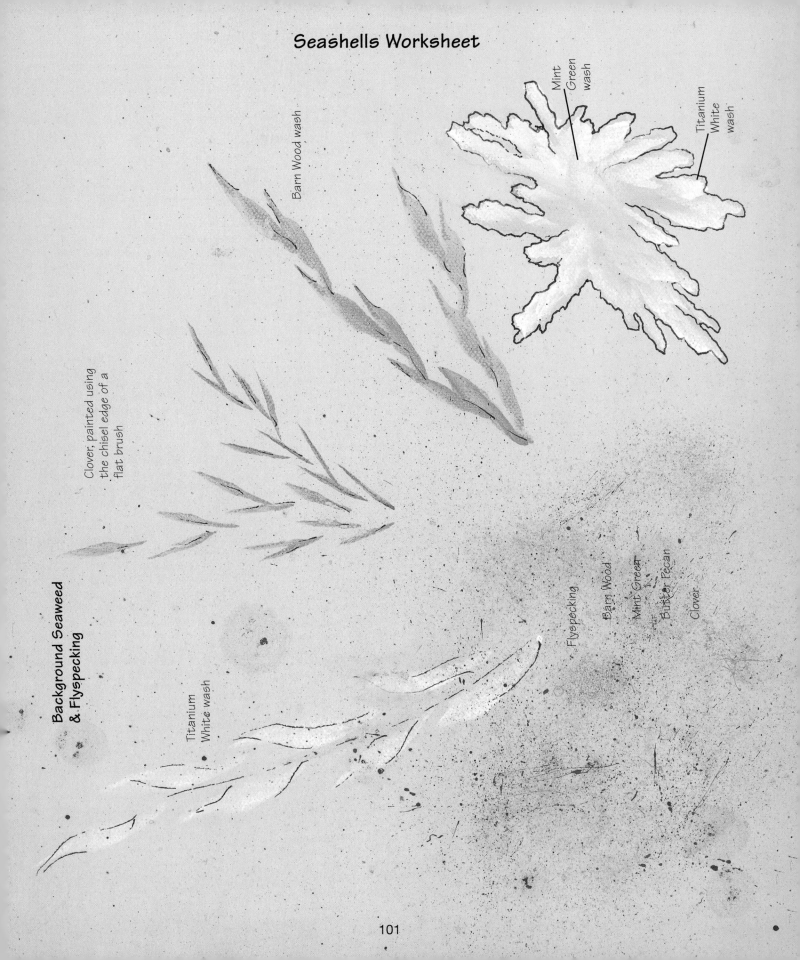

Mint
Green
wash

Titanium
White
wash

Barn Wood wash

Clover, painted using
the chisel edge of a
flat brush

**Background Seaweed
& Flyspecking**

Titanium
White wash

Flyspecking

Barn Wood

Mint Green

Butter Pecan

Clover

Seashells Worksheet

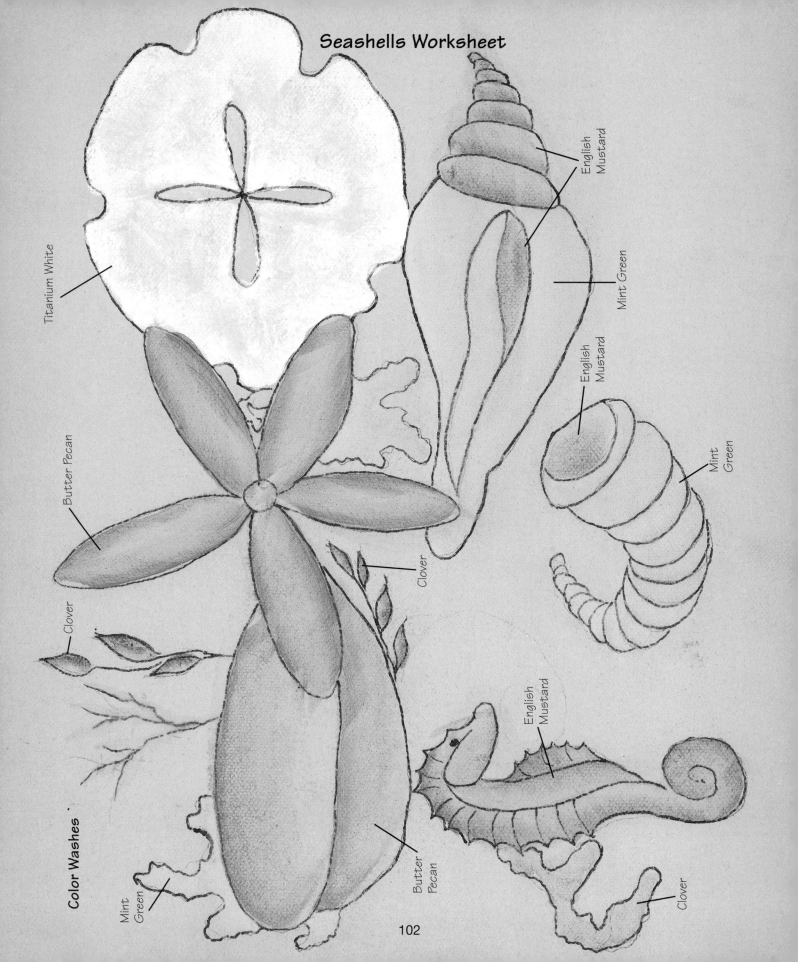

Titanium White

English Mustard

Mint Green

English Mustard

English Mustard

Mint Green

Butter Pecan

Clover

Clover

Color Washes

Mint Green

Butter Pecan

English Mustard

Clover

Seashells Worksheet

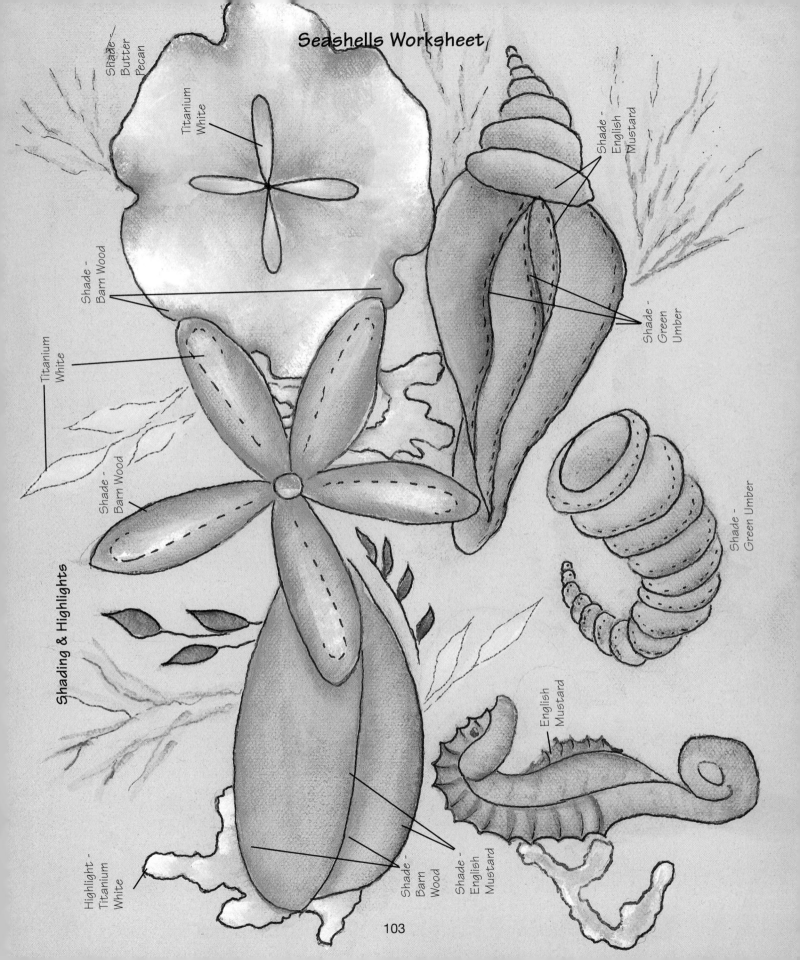

Shade - Butter Pecan

Titanium White

Shade - English Mustard

Shade - Barn Wood

Shade - Green Umber

Titanium White

Shade - Barn Wood

Shade - Green Umber

Shading & Highlights

Shade - Green Umber

Highlight - Titanium White

Shade - Barn Wood

Shade - English Mustard

English Mustard

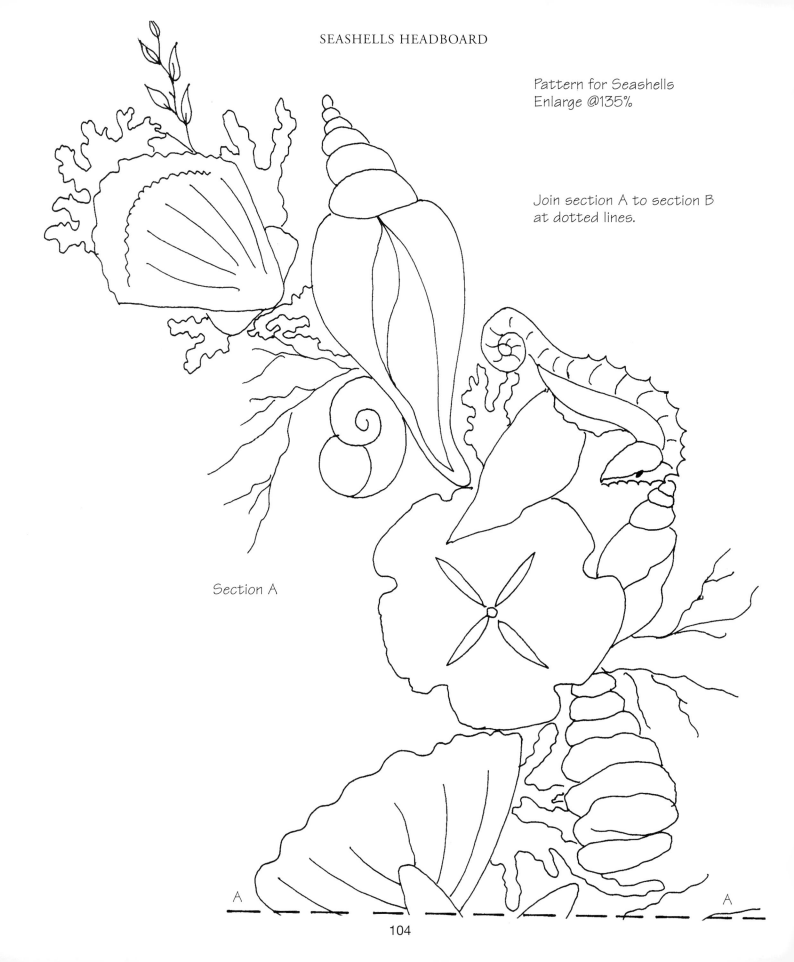

Pattern for Seashells
Enlarge @135%

Join section A to section B
at dotted lines.

Section A

A

A

Reverse and repeat from center line
for second half of pattern.

center

center line

Section B

B

B

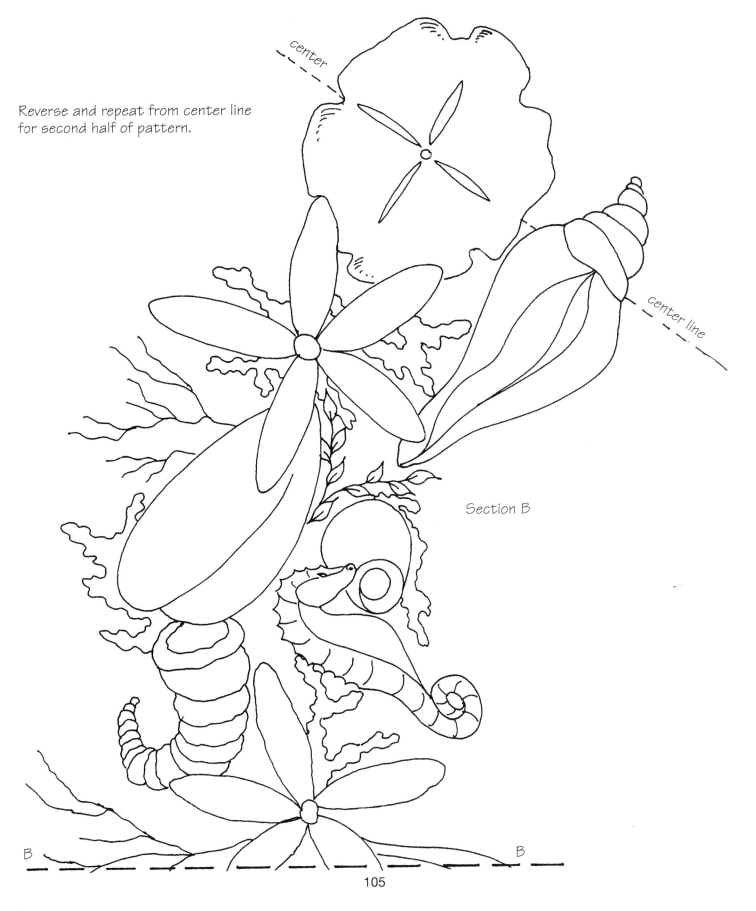

Lemon Kitchen Shelf

Little wall shelves are easy to find at garage sales and "junktique" and thrift stores. When I found this one, I immediately saw lemons on it. Talk about easy! Just give this technique a try.

My shelf came with peeling white paint, so I simply sanded it to remove the loose flakes and painted the design. I've included instructions for duplicating the distressed look.

Instructions follow on page 108

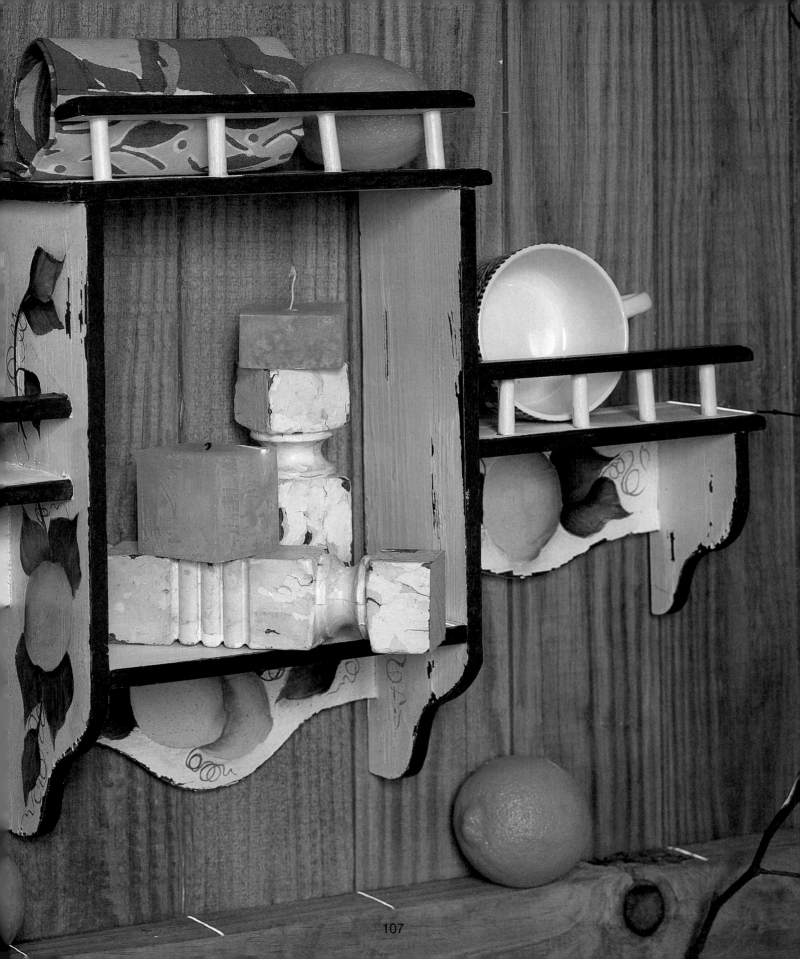

PALETTE OF COLORS

Artist Pigment Acrylic Paints:

Burnt Sienna

Burnt Umber

Green Dark

Green Light

Green Medium

Payne's Gray

Titanium White

Acrylic Craft Paints:

Lemon Custard

Navy Blue

Old Ivy

Wicker White

BRUSHES
Flat - #20

Liner - #1

Old toothbrush (for flyspecking)

Sponge brush for painting surface

SURFACE
Wooden wall plate shelf, flea market find

OTHER SUPPLIES
In addition to the Basic Supplies listed on page 29, you will need:

Painting Medium - Blending medium

Waterbase varnish

Optional: Sanding block or medium grade sandpaper

PREPARATION
1. Sand the shelf. Wipe with a tack cloth.
2. Paint with two or more coats of Wicker White, letting the paint dry between each coat.
3. *Option:* For a distressed look, use a sanding block or medium grade sandpaper to lift the paint off here and there. Wipe with a tack cloth.
4. Neatly trace and transfer the design.
5. Sideload a wet #20 flat brush with Payne's Gray and float color around the lemon motifs. See the step-by-step photos that follow for a picture of this.

PAINTING THE DESIGN
Leaves:

Paint the leaves under the lemons, following the instructions for "Painting a Quick & Easy Leaf" and the illustrations on the Leaf Worksheet as shown on pages 60-61.

Lemons:

See the Lemon Worksheet.
1. Neatly undercoat the lemons with three or four coats of Lemon Custard. Let dry and cure.
2. Double-load a #20 flat brush with blending medium and Burnt Sienna. Float shading on the lemons as shown on the worksheet. Let dry and cure.
3. Repeat the shading for more depth. Let dry.
4. Load a toothbrush with Burnt Sienna thinned with water. Flyspeck the lemons.

Curlicues:

1. Thin Green Dark with water to an ink-like consistency and fill the #1 liner brush.
2. Hold the brush with the handle pointing straight up and slowly paint the curls and swirls. Let the paint dry and cure.

FINISHING

1. Paint trim on shelf with Navy Blue to accent, as desired. Let dry and cure.
2. Varnish with two or more coats of waterbase varnish. ❏

Left Side - Top

Lemon Patterns
Actual Size

Top

Top Right

Center

Painting a Lemon, Step by Step

THE BACKGROUND

1. Sideload a wet brush with a little Payne's Gray.

2. Float the color around the outside of the design.

THE LEMONS

3. Undercoat lemon shapes with Lemon Custard. Apply three coats and let dry between coats. After the third coat is painted, let dry and cure.

4. Double-load brush with Burnt Sienna and blending medium. Blend the brush on the palette so the paint color flows across the brush from dark to medium to light.

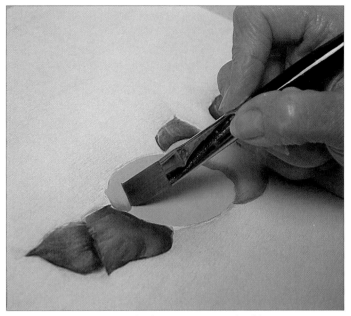

5. Float Burnt Sienna shading at stem end of lemon.

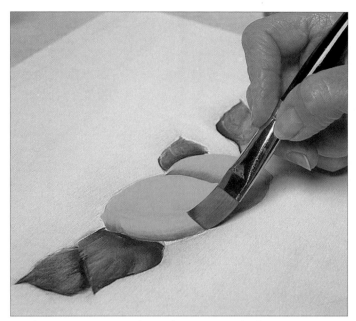

6. Float Burnt Sienna along the curve to shade.

FLYSPECKING

7. Load a toothbrush with thinned paint.

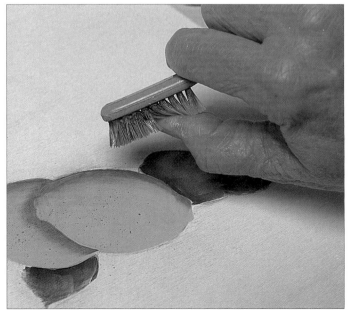

8. Holding the loaded toothbrush above the surface, run your thumb over the bristles to release tiny specks of paint.

Finishing Details, Step by Step

CURLICUES

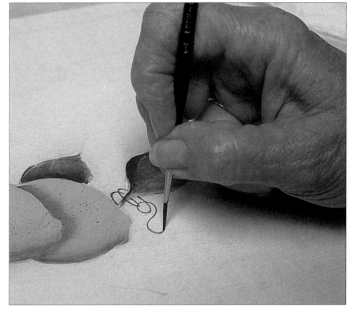

9. Paint curlicues, using a liner brush. Hold the brush perpendicular to the surface.

Lemon Worksheet

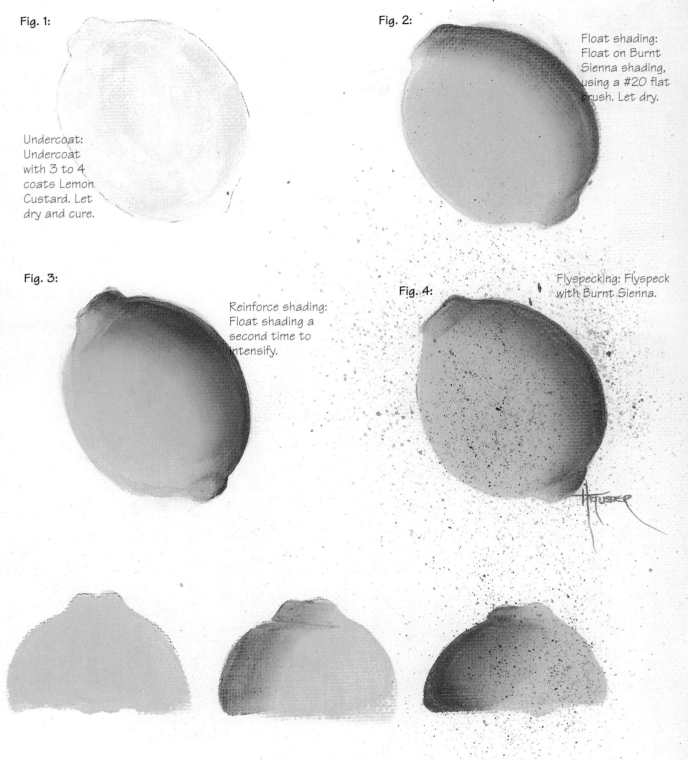

Fig. 1:

Undercoat: Undercoat with 3 to 4 coats Lemon Custard. Let dry and cure.

Fig. 2:

Float shading: Float on Burnt Sienna shading, using a #20 flat brush. Let dry.

Fig. 3:

Reinforce shading: Float shading a second time to intensify.

Fig. 4:

Flyspecking: Flyspeck with Burnt Sienna.

Lemon Patterns
Actual Size

Right - Inside

Left - Outside

Left - Inside

Lemon Patterns
Actual Size

Bottom -
Left Side

Bottom - Right Side

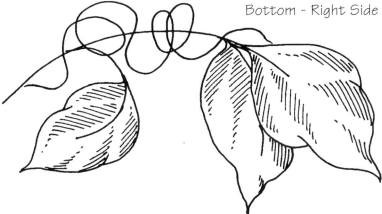

Woodland Ferns Table

This wonderful coffee table was in really bad shape when I got it. I paid very little for it, but I could tell by its lines that it would be charming when finished.

Some of the ferns in the background are painted; others are created with a stamp. The two pages of the Fern Worksheet show the painting techniques.

Instructions follow on page 118

PALETTE OF COLORS

Artist Pigment Acrylic Paints:

Green Dark

Green Light

Green Umber

Raw Sienna

Acrylic Craft Paints:

Titanium White

Barn Wood

Clover

English Mustard

BRUSHES

Flat - #14

Liners - #1, #10/0

Filbert - #20

Sponge brushes, 1" & 2", for painting surface

SURFACE

Wooden coffee table, unfinished or flea market find

OTHER SUPPLIES

In addition to the Basic Supplies listed on page 29, you will need:

Glazing medium

Fern motif foam stamp, 4"

Satin waterbase varnish

Latex wall paint, eggshell finish, for painting table: off-white, barnwood gray

PREPARATION

1. Clean the table, if needed.
2. Sand the table with fine grade sandpaper. Wipe with a tack cloth.
3. Using a 2" wide sponge brush, apply two or more coats of barnwood gray latex wall paint to the top of the table. Using a 1" sponge brush, paint the legs with two or more coats of off-white latex wall paint. Allow the paint to dry between each coat. Let the paint dry and cure.
4. Rub with a piece of brown paper bag with no printing on it to smooth the surface.
5. Neatly trace and transfer the design.

PAINTING THE DESIGN

Shadow Ferns:

These shadow ferns are painted and stamped with very thin paint to create the background. See the Fern Worksheet #1.

1. Make a very thin watery wash of Titanium White (a touch of paint + a lot of water).
2. Paint the stems of the leafy ferns with a liner brush.
3. Use a #14 flat brush to make s-strokes to create the leafy segments.
4. Paint the thin-lined ferns using the liner brush full of thinned paint or the chisel edge of the flat brush.
5. Use the same watery paint with the foam stamp to create other shadow ferns.

Fern #1:

See the Fern Worksheet #2.

1. Using a liner brush full of thinned Raw Sienna, paint the stems.
2. Double-load a filbert with Green Light and Clover. Touch, press, pull slightly, and lift to create the leafy segments. TIP: If you have trouble double-loading, put down Green Light first, then shade it while wet with a touch of Clover.
3. Shade with Green Umber.
4. Highlight with Titanium White.
5. Enhance the leafy segments with just a touch of Green Dark.

Fern #2:

See the Fern Worksheet #3.

1. Using a filbert brush, undercoat the fern with Clover.
2. Brush on a little glazing medium. Shade the edges with Green Dark.

Continued on page 123

Fern Worksheet #1

Shadow Ferns:

Paint with a watery wash of Titanium White.

Use the chisel edge of a flat brush to paint some of ferns.

Use a foam stamp with a fern motif to stamp other ferns.

Fern Worksheet #2

Shade with Green Umber. Highlight with Titanium White. Enhance with a touch of Green Dark.

Paint stems with Raw Sienna. Paint the leafy segments using a filbert double-loaded with Green Light and Clover.

Fern #1

Fern Worksheet #3

Highlight with
Titanium White.
Brush English
Mustard here and
there to add
touches of color.

A finished fern.

Fern #2

Using a filbert
brush, undercoat
the fern with Clover.
Brush on a little
glazing
medium. Shade
the edges with
Green Dark.

Enhance with
Green Light.

Fern Worksheet #4

Apply glazing medium. Brush Green Dark to shade. Paint the stem with Green Dark. Highlight with Green Light.

Fern #3
Undercoat with Clover. Let dry.

continued from page 118

3. Enhance with Green Light.
4. Highlight with Titanium White.
5. Brush English Mustard here and there to add touches of color.

Fern #3:
See the Fern Worksheet #4.
1. Undercoat the with Clover. Let dry.

2. Apply glazing medium. Brush Green Dark to shade. Paint the stem with Green Dark.
3. Highlight the edges with Green Light. Let the painting dry and cure.

FINISHING
Varnish with two or three coats of waterbase varnish. ❏

Patterns for Ferns
Enlarge @ 240%

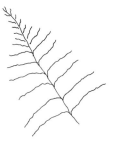

Patterns for Ferns
Enlarge @ 160%

Patterns for Ferns
Enlarge @ 160%

By the Sea Tray

Pen and ink color wash is so fast and easy that it can easily be done in an afternoon. Yet the results are so lovely it will look like you have spent days perfecting it. I've given you two of my favorite shell designs that can be created on a number of different surfaces.

This tray can be used almost anywhere — in the bathroom to hold guest towels or toiletries; in a guest room; in the kitchen or dining room used for serving while entertaining; or even placed on a plate holder and used as art.

PALETTE OF COLORS

Artist Pigment Acrylic Paints:

Aqua

Burnt Carmine

Ice Green Light

Light Red Oxide

Prussian Blue

Warm White

Yellow Ochre

SURFACE
Unfinished wooden tray, 12" x 16"

BRUSHES
Flats - #2, #8, #10, #14

Flat wash brush - 1"

Sponge brush, 1", for painting surface

OTHER SUPPLIES
In addition to the Basic Supplies listed on page 29, you will need:

Glazing medium

Permanent black ink marking pen with fine point

Acrylic matte-finish spray sealer

Instructions on page 128

PREPARATION

1. Sand the wooden tray with fine grade sandpaper. Wipe with a tack cloth.
2. Mix equal amounts of Warm White paint and Glazing Medium to create a stain.
3. Using the sponge brush, brush this mixture onto the tray surface, then immediately wipe it off with a soft cloth. Let dry. Apply a second coat, if desired. Let dry.
4. Rub surface with a piece of brown paper bag with no printing on it to smooth the nap of the wood.
5. The sky and the sand on the background are created with washes of color. To make a wash, apply just a touch of color into the Glazing Medium. Apply this color with the 1" flat wash brush. Use a light touch and blend quickly, as you don't have much time. It is always good to practice washes on a piece of prepared wood before going to the actual surface. It is quick and easy to do, but a little practice beforehand will build your confidence. For the sky some areas were washed with a glazing mixture made with Aqua paint. Other areas were washed with a mixture made with a touch of Prussian Blue and a touch of Yellow Ochre. The sand is wash of all three colors. Allow to dry before proceeding.
6. Neatly trace the design onto a sheet of tracing paper. Trace only the outside lines of the design. Turn the paper over and go over the lines on the back with a #2 graphite pencil. Do not scribble all over the back! Neatly center the design on the tray. Using a stylus or a pencil, retrace the lines. The graphite lines will transfer the pattern to the tray.

PAINTING THE DESIGN

See the "By the Sea" Worksheets for painting details. Use flat brushes to apply the washes that are appropriate to the size of the design.

Shells & Coral:

1. Using the permanent black ink marking pen, ink all the outside lines of the design. Allow to dry. Erase any graphite lines that show.
2. Make washes of all the colors listed except Warm White. To do this, add just a touch of color to the Glazing Medium.
3. Paint the shell by washing first with Light Red Oxide. Add a second wash of Light Red Oxide in shaded areas. Add a wash of Prussian Blue in areas shown on the worksheet. Let dry.
4. Paint the coral by washing some areas with Yellow Ochre, some with Ice Green Light, and some areas with a wash mix of Yellow Ochre + Burnt Carmine.
5. Add a second layer of shading to the coral. In the Yellow Ochre area, add a shading wash of Yellow Ochre + Burnt Carmine. In the Ice Green Light areas, add another layer of Ice Green Light. In the remainder of the areas add a wash of Prussian Blue. See worksheet for example. Allow to dry.
6. Ink the dots and the slash lines over the dried color to create definition. Work neatly and carefully. Let dry.

Lettering:

1. Outline the lettering with the permanent black ink marker.
2. Add diagonal lines to create the shading. Let dry.

FINISHING

1. Mist with many coats of spray varnish. Let dry.
2. Rub with a piece of brown paper bag with no printing on it to smooth the surface.
3. Apply a final coat of varnish. ❏

Lettering Pattern
Actual Size

By the Sea Worksheet #1

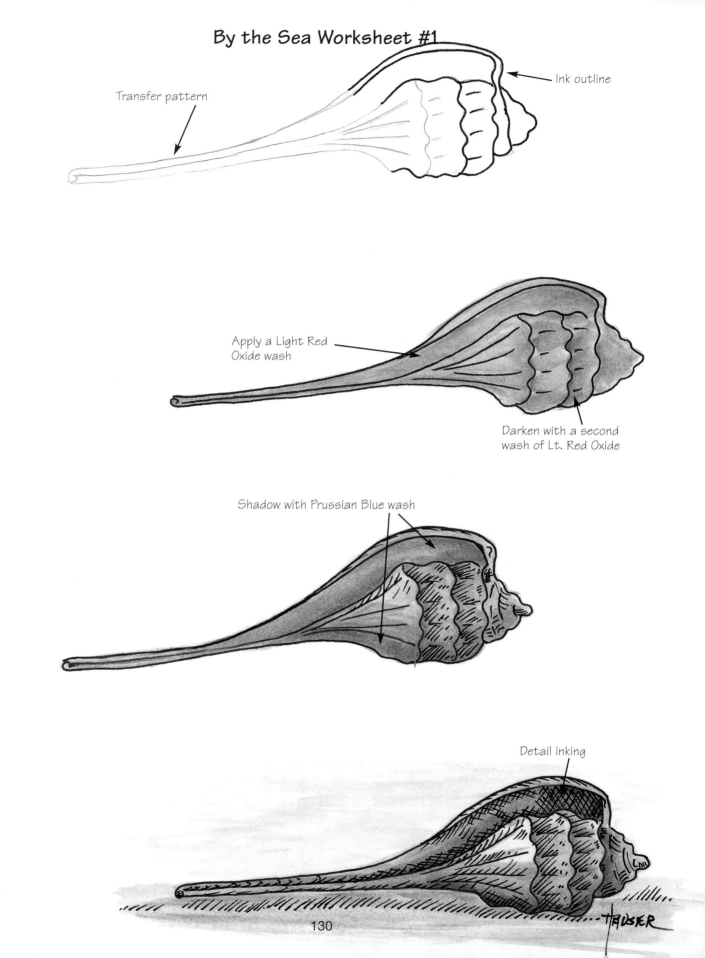

Transfer pattern

Ink outline

Apply a Light Red Oxide wash

Darken with a second wash of Lt. Red Oxide

Shadow with Prussian Blue wash

Detail inking

130

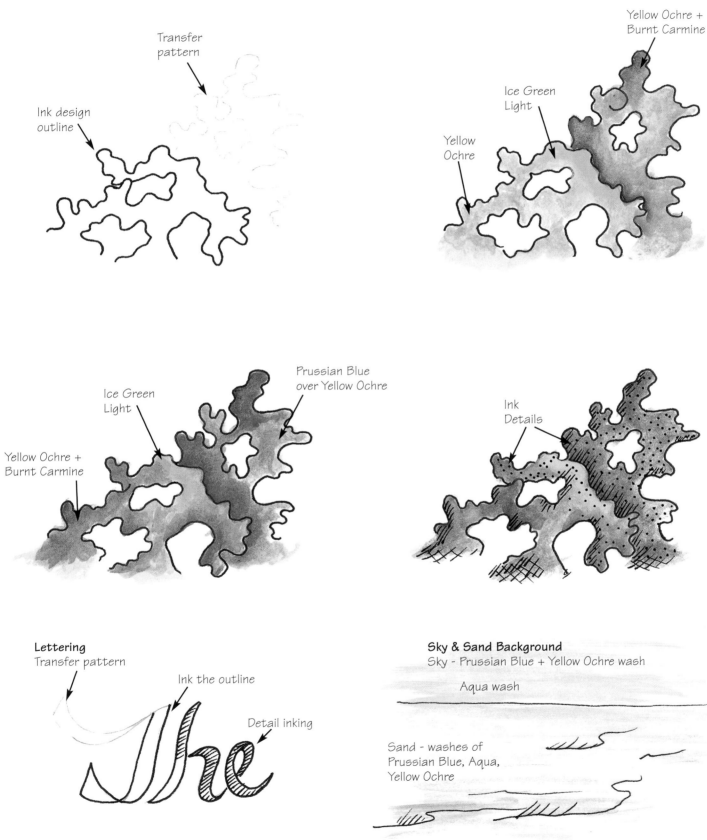

Transfer pattern

Ink design outline

Yellow Ochre + Burnt Carmine

Ice Green Light

Yellow Ochre

Ice Green Light

Prussian Blue over Yellow Ochre

Yellow Ochre + Burnt Carmine

Ink Details

Lettering
Transfer pattern

Ink the outline

Detail inking

Sky & Sand Background
Sky - Prussian Blue + Yellow Ochre wash

Aqua wash

Sand - washes of Prussian Blue, Aqua, Yellow Ochre

131

Shells & Coral Pattern
Actual Size

Bonus Pattern

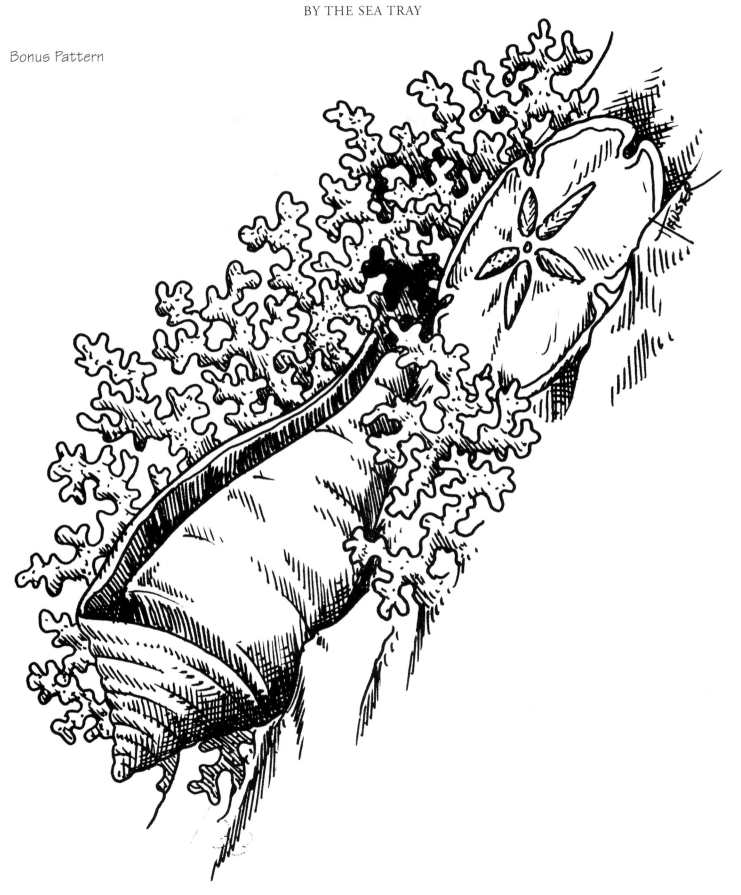

Springtime Birdhouse Clock

Springtime is such a beautiful time of the year. By using this design on the face of a clock, you can fill your kitchen, or any room, with a touch of spring year round. Try painting this design to coordinate various accessories in the kitchen or throughout your home.

PALETTE OF COLORS

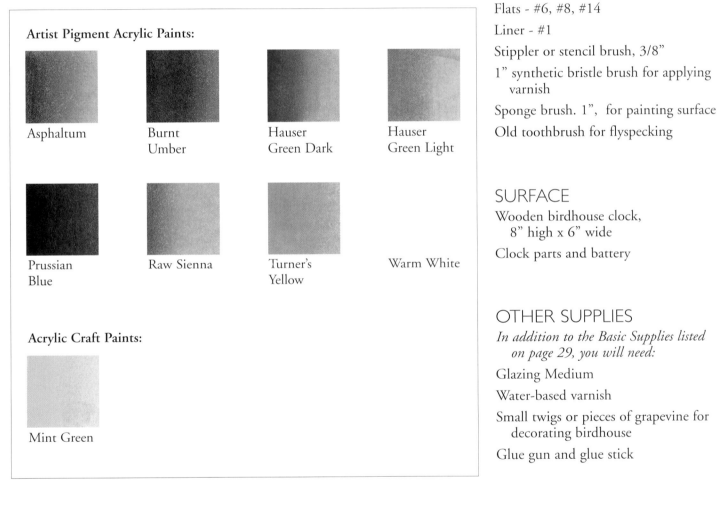

Artist Pigment Acrylic Paints:

Asphaltum

Burnt Umber

Hauser Green Dark

Hauser Green Light

Prussian Blue

Raw Sienna

Turner's Yellow

Warm White

Acrylic Craft Paints:

Mint Green

BRUSHES

Flats - #6, #8, #14

Liner - #1

Stippler or stencil brush, 3/8"

1" synthetic bristle brush for applying varnish

Sponge brush. 1", for painting surface

Old toothbrush for flyspecking

SURFACE

Wooden birdhouse clock, 8" high x 6" wide

Clock parts and battery

OTHER SUPPLIES

In addition to the Basic Supplies listed on page 29, you will need:

Glazing Medium

Water-based varnish

Small twigs or pieces of grapevine for decorating birdhouse

Glue gun and glue stick

PREPARATION

1. Sand the clock with fine grade sandpaper. Wipe with a tack cloth.
2. Using the 1" sponge brush, apply two coats of Mint Green to the base, roof and the backside of the clock. Do not paint the front of the clock, it will be left the natural wood color.
3. Neatly trace the design onto tracing paper. Transfer the design to the front of the clock onto the raw wood surface using gray transfer paper.

Continued on next page

Birdhouse Worksheet #1

1

For background around nest, use Asphaltum and glazing medium. Blend.

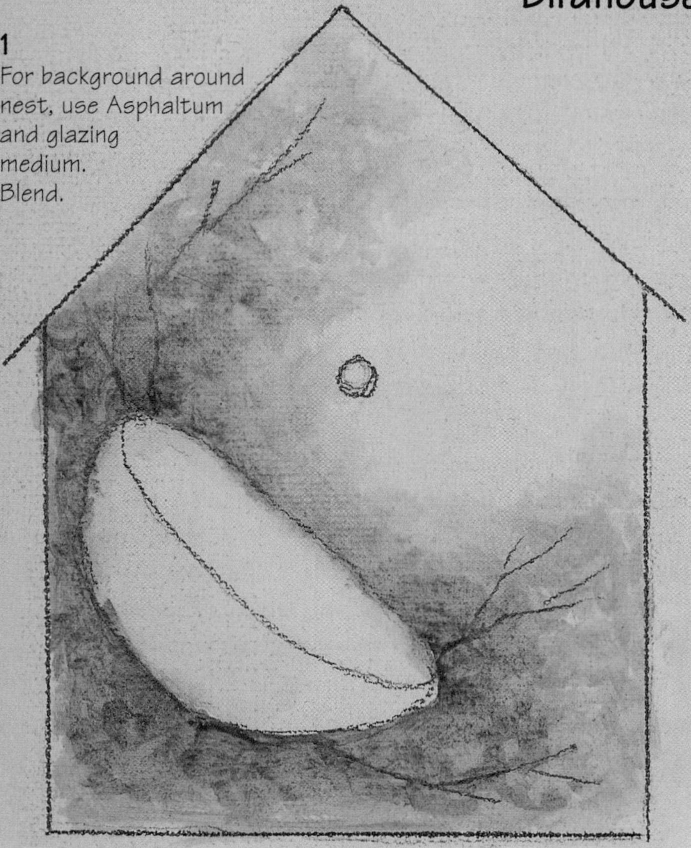

2

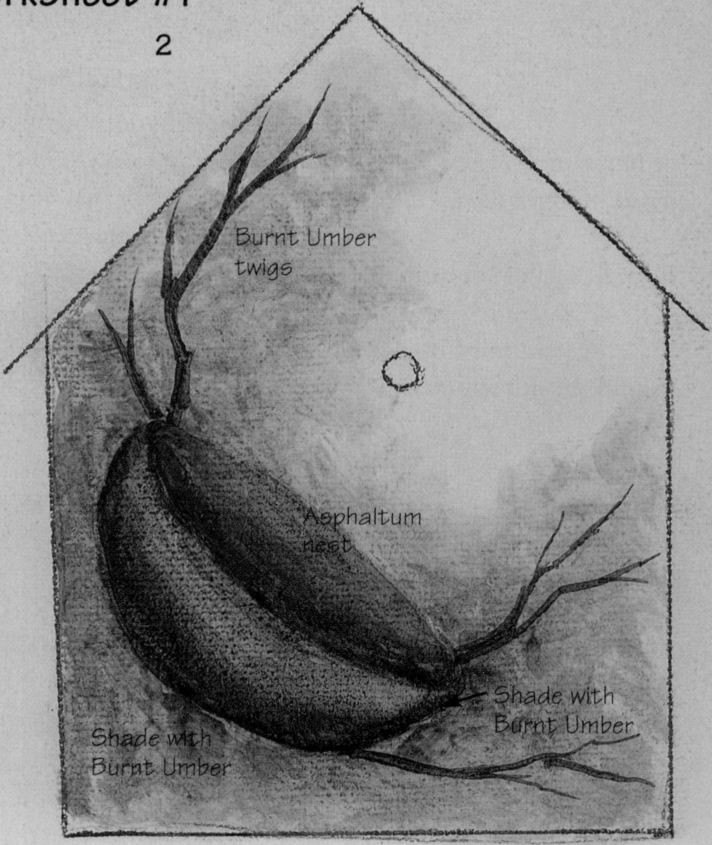

Burnt Umber twigs

Asphaltum nest

Shade with Burnt Umber

Shade with Burnt Umber

3

Mint Green eggs Foliage - dab on Hauser Gr. Light Warm White lines on nest

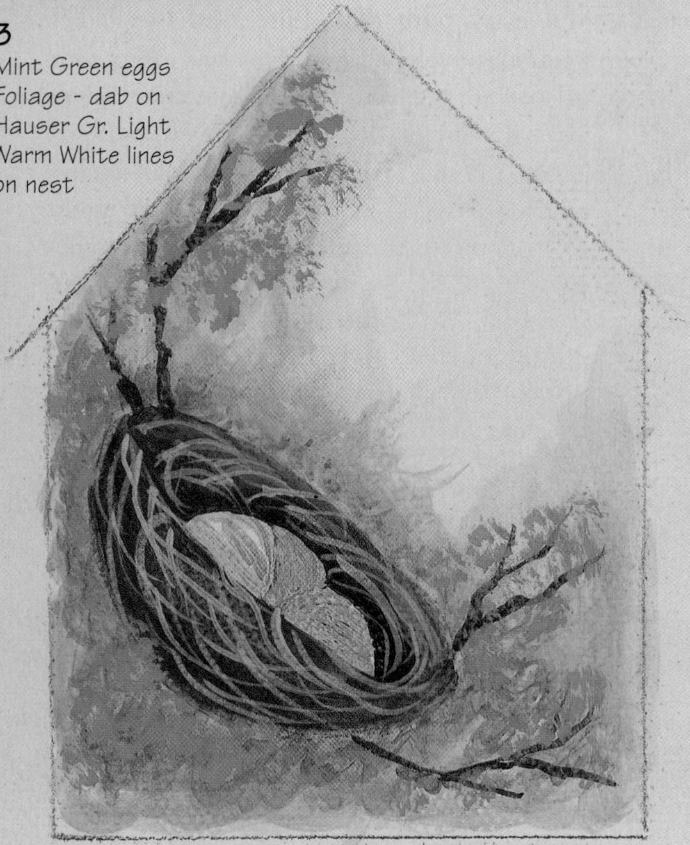

4

Raw Sienna lines on nest

Birdhouse Worksheet #2

5

Eggs - shade with
floated Burnt Umber
+ Pr. Blue
Foliage - dab on
Hauser Gr.
Dark

6

Foliage - highlight
with Mint Green
Flyspeck with
Asphaltum

Eat, Drink & Bee Merry Plate

Using a tool called a "Spouncer", which is a round sponge attached to a wooden stick, you can quickly and very attractively create a real buzz. These bees are delightful on any surface. I picked up this wooden tray at a garage sale. It can be hung on the wall or placed in a plate holder as a piece of art or used as a serving piece when lined with a clear glass plate.

PALETTE OF COLORS

Artist Pigment Acrylic Paints:

Asphaltum
Hauser

Hauser Green
Medium

Medium
Yellow

Pure Black

Titanium
White

Turner's
Yellow

**Acrylic
Craft
Paints:**

Licorice

BRUSHES
Flats - #2, #12

Liner - #1

Sponge brush, 1", for painting surface

Old toothbrush for flyspecking

5/8" sponge dabbing tool, or 5/8" round sponge

Continued on page 142

SURFACE

Wooden plate, 15" dia.

OTHER SUPPLIES

In addition to the Basic Supplies listed on page 29, you will need:

Glazing Medium

Pearlizing medium

Water-based varnish

PREPARATION

1. Sand the tray, if needed. Wipe with a tack cloth.
2. Make a very light glaze by mixing a little Asphaltum in glazing medium. Apply to the center area to stain the plate. You will need to stain approximately a 9" diameter area. Don't worry about being neat or precise, the paint border colors will cover the edge of this.
3. Beginning from outside edge of plate, paint border of color in this order:
   a) 1/8" border of Turner's Yellow,
   b) 1-1/2" border of Licorice,
   c) 1/8" border of Turner's Yellow,
   d) 1-1/2" border of Hauser Green Medium,
   e) 1/4" border of Licorice.
   When painting these borders of color, tape off or make a mask to help keep edges crisp. Allow to dry.
4. Using a toothbrush or flyspecking tool and thinned Licorice, flyspeck the entire surface. Allow to dry.
5. Neatly trace and transfer the design with white graphite paper.

PAINTING THE DESIGN

See the Bees Worksheet for painting details.

Bees:

1. Fill the round sponge tool with Medium Yellow. Dab it up and down many times on a rag to remove some of the excess paint. Dab two times (as shown on the worksheet) to form the upper and lower portion of the body. When I press, I wiggle the dauber back and forth just a little bit. This motion will also help to make the larger circle for the back part of the body.
2. Pick up Asphaltum on the edge of the sponge. Dab up and down on the palette a few times to blend the colors. Blot on the rag. Shade the upper and lower part of the body as shown on the worksheet.
3. Pick up a tiny bit of Pure Black on the edge of the sponge. Dab up and down on the palette a few times to blend the colors. Apply it to the bee's body to shade the body between the sections and a the back end, as shown on the worksheet.
4. Fill the #1 liner brush with thinned Pure Black. Paint the wiggly lines across the body, as shown on the worksheet.
5. Make a gray mixture of Titanium White plus Pure Black (3:1). Paint the head, the feelers and the legs with this mixture. Let dry.
6. Using your #12 flat brush, apply thinned Pearlizing Medium to create the wings as shown on the worksheet. Note: Any iridescent white (or even thinned white paint) will work for the wings. Let dry.

FINISHING

1. Using the liner brush and Licorice paint, letter "Eat, Drink, and Bee Merry" on the green border section. If you are not comfortable lettering with a brush, you can use a permanent ink marker. Allow to dry.
2. Varnish with two or more coats of water-based varnish.
   ❏

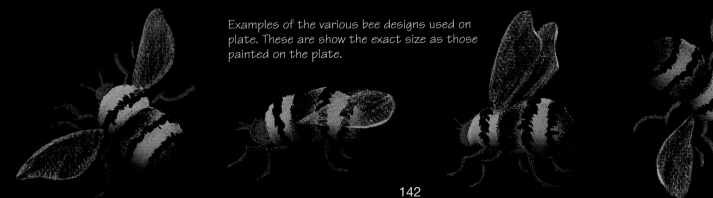

Examples of the various bee designs used on plate. These are show the exact size as those painted on the plate.

Bee Worksheet #1

1
Medium Yellow applied with a sponge
Shade with Asphaltum

2
Dab a bigger circle using Medium
Yellow. Shade the bottom with
Asphaltum.

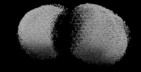

3
Shade between the body sections
with Pure Black

4
Shade back of body with Pure Black

5
Using liner brush and Pure Black,
make the wiggly lines across body.

6
Paint head, feelers, and legs with a
gray mixture of Pure Black and
Titanium White.

7
Paint wings using the #12 flat brush
using pearlizing medium, iridescent
paint, or thinned white paint.

Plate Border Pattern
Actual Size

Pyracantha Birdcage & Plant Stand

You see something old and beaten-up, and you love it. You can't decide what you'll do with it, but you just can't do without it. Buy it! You just never know what kind of treasure it will become.

This old birdcage was in horrible shape, but I could see that, once restored, it would have possibilities. The little plant stand was charming. Perhaps, once upon a time, it may have been a piece of doll furniture.

PALETTE OF COLORS

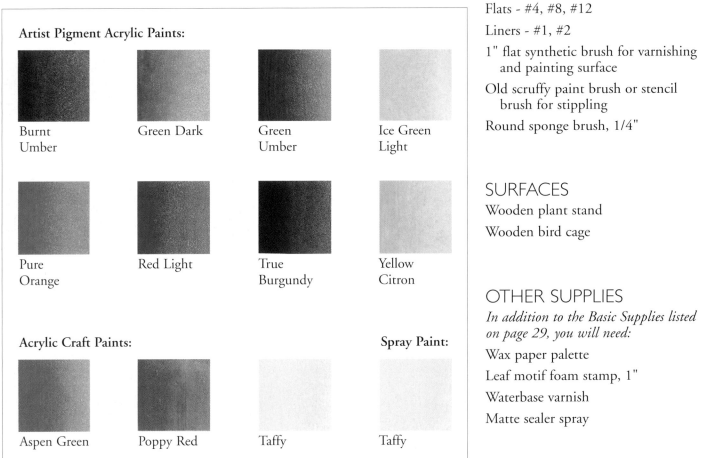

Artist Pigment Acrylic Paints:

Burnt Umber

Green Dark

Green Umber

Ice Green Light

Pure Orange

Red Light

True Burgundy

Yellow Citron

Acrylic Craft Paints:

Aspen Green

Poppy Red

Taffy

Spray Paint:

Taffy

BRUSHES

Flats - #4, #8, #12

Liners - #1, #2

1" flat synthetic brush for varnishing and painting surface

Old scruffy paint brush or stencil brush for stippling

Round sponge brush, 1/4"

SURFACES

Wooden plant stand

Wooden bird cage

OTHER SUPPLIES

In addition to the Basic Supplies listed on page 29, you will need:

Wax paper palette

Leaf motif foam stamp, 1"

Waterbase varnish

Matte sealer spray

Instructions follow on page 148.
Birdcage pictured on page 149.

PREPARATION

Plant Stand:

1. Sand with fine grade sandpaper. Wipe with a tack cloth.
2. Apply two coats of Taffy, using a 1" synthetic brush or a sponge brush. Allow the paint to dry between each coat.
3. Trace and transfer the design using gray graphite.
4. Use a ruler and pencil to lightly mark the outline of a square on the top, using the photo as a guide.

Birdcage:

1. Clean the metal with a stiff wire brush.
2. Sand the wood trim. Wipe with a tack cloth.
3. Spray with Taffy. Let dry.
4. Sand the wood with fine grade sandpaper for a distressed look.
5. Trace and transfer the design using gray graphite.

PAINTING THE DESIGN

See the Pyracantha Worksheet.

Leaves:

Use a foam stamp to create the leaves.

1. Brush Aspen Green on the stamp, using a #8 flat brush.
2. Press the stamp to the surface. Stamp one or two leaves at a time. This undercoat will be somewhat transparent and may appear messy at this point. Allow to dry.
3. Use a #12 flat brush to shade the base of each leaf with a Green Umber float.
4. Using a float of Green Umber, create the split tip that is characteristic of pyracantha leaves.
5. Highlight the right side of the leaves with a Yellow Citron float.
6. Accent the left side with a True Burgundy float.

Berries:

Paint the berries with the 1/4" round sponge brush. Practice on a brown paper bag.

1. Load the 1/4" round sponge brush with Poppy Red. Blot on a rag.
2. Stamp or dab it on the surface to make a berry. Twist the sponge brush slightly as you apply it to the surface. Allow

this undercoat to dry completely.

3. Pick up True Burgundy on one side of the round brush and Red Light on the other side. Dab on the wax palette, turning it slightly as you dab, to blend the colors.
4. Press the loaded sponge brush over the undercoat, twisting it as you press. Let dry.
5. Accent some of the berries with a Pure Orange float. Let dry.
6. Paint a "star" on the blossom ends of some berries.

Stems:

1. Using the tip of a #2 liner brush, undercoat the stems in Aspen Green.
2. Using a #4 flat brush, shade the stems on the left with a Burnt Umber float.
3. Highlight along the right side with a Yellow Citron float.

Moss:

1. Using an old scruffy brush or stencil brush, stipple a small section of Green Umber along the stem in several areas of the design.
2. Highlight the moss with dabs of Ice Green Light, using the same scruffy brush.

Curlicues:

Add curlicues to the design, using a liner brush and thinned Green Umber. Let dry.

FINISHING

Plant Stand:

1. Paint the outline of the square on the top with Green Dark.
2. Paint legs and sides with Green Dark. Let dry.
3. Sand lightly for a distressed look. Wipe away dust.
4. Apply two coats of waterbase varnish. Let dry between coats.

Birdcage:

Spray with matte sealer. ❏

Pyracantha Worksheet

Leaves

Stamp leaf with Aspen Green.

Shade with Green Umber.

Create the split tip of the leaf with Green Umber.

Highlight right side with Yellow Citron.

Accent with True Burgundy.

Berries

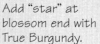

Load round sponge brush with Red Poppy. Press on surface.

Load sponge brush with True Burgundy and Red Light.

Press and twist slightly on surface.

Highlight some with Pure Orange.

Add "star" at blossom end with True Burgundy.

Stem

Highlight with Yellow Citron.

Undercoat with Aspen Green.

Shade with Burnt Umber.

Moss

Dab with Green Umber.

Dab with Ice Green.

Dab moss on stem in a few places.

Plant Stand Top
Actual Size

Birdcage Front
Actual Size

Birdcage Side
Actual Size

Pattern for Holly Bucket
Actual Size
Instructions on page 124

Holly Bucket

Galvanized buckets — both new and used — are easy to find, and their uses are many. This one is decorated for Christmas with simple holly, leaves, and ribbon.

PALETTE OF COLORS

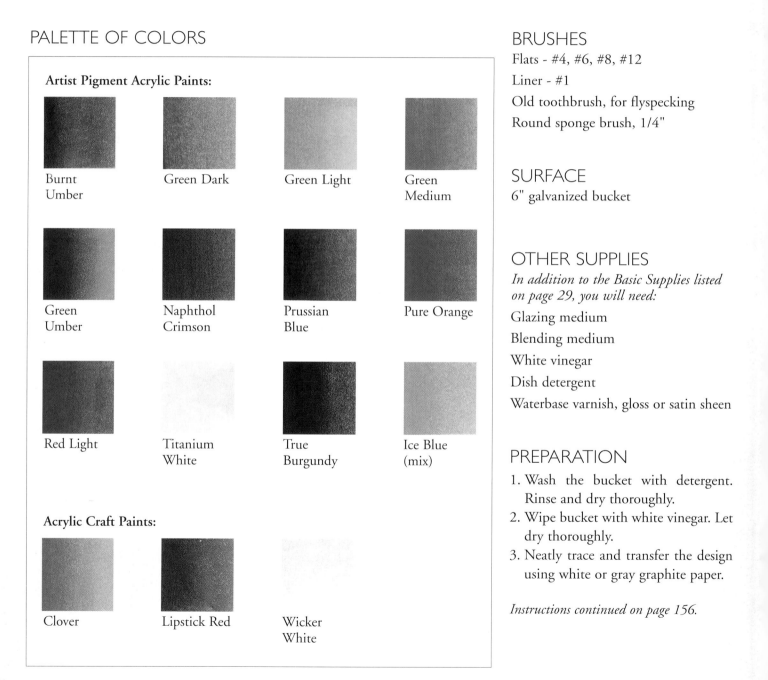

Artist Pigment Acrylic Paints:

Burnt Umber

Green Dark

Green Light

Green Medium

Green Umber

Naphthol Crimson

Prussian Blue

Pure Orange

Red Light

Titanium White

True Burgundy

Ice Blue (mix)

Acrylic Craft Paints:

Clover

Lipstick Red

Wicker White

BRUSHES

Flats - #4, #6, #8, #12

Liner - #1

Old toothbrush, for flyspecking

Round sponge brush, 1/4"

SURFACE

6" galvanized bucket

OTHER SUPPLIES

In addition to the Basic Supplies listed on page 29, you will need:

Glazing medium

Blending medium

White vinegar

Dish detergent

Waterbase varnish, gloss or satin sheen

PREPARATION

1. Wash the bucket with detergent. Rinse and dry thoroughly.
2. Wipe bucket with white vinegar. Let dry thoroughly.
3. Neatly trace and transfer the design using white or gray graphite paper.

Instructions continued on page 156.

PAINTING THE DESIGN

Holly Leaves:

Paint the holly leaves in dark, medium, and light values. Leaves at the back of the design are darkest, and those leaves close to the front are light. See the Holly Worksheet.

1. Neatly undercoat the leaves in Clover. Let dry and cure.

2. Apply shadows at the bases of the leaves by floating on Green Umber. Let dry.

3. To complete the dark leaves, apply a small amount of blending medium and Green Umber at the base. Apply Green Dark, then a little Green Medium, and then an ice blue mix (Titanium White + tiny touch of Prussian Blue + tiny touch Burnt Umber). Wipe the brush and blend using a light touch.

4. To complete the medium leaves, apply a small amount of blending medium. Apply Green Umber and, above that, a little Green Medium. Above that, apply a little Green Light; above that, apply Titanium White. Wipe the brush and blend.

5. To complete the light leaves, apply a small amount of blending medium. Apply Green Umber at the base. Apply a tiny bit of Green Dark, Green Light above that, Titanium White above that. Wipe the brush and blend.

Berries:

Paint the berries with a 1/4" round sponge brush. Practice on a brown paper bag. See the Holly Worksheet.

1. Press the 1/4" round sponge brush several times in Naphthol Crimson. Blot on a damp rag or paper towel. Press on the surface and lift to create the berry. Let the berry dry.

2. Pick up True Burgundy on the edge of the sponge brush. Press over the undercoated berry to shade.

3. Pick up some Pure Orange or Red Light on the sponge brush (use Pure Orange on some, Red Light on others).

Highlight the berries.

Ribbon:

See the Ribbon Worksheet.

1. Using a small flat brush, carefully and neatly undercoat the ribbon with Wicker White. Let dry and cure thoroughly.

2. Paint with Red Light and Naphthol Crimson, using the worksheet as a guide. Let dry and cure.

3. Shade the ribbon with True Burgundy, using the worksheet as a guide. Let dry and cure.

Trim:

1. To mark the top band, measure 3/4" down from the top of the bucket, marking the distance with a pencil. Connect the dots to form a line.

2. Use the width of a #12 flat brush to paint the sections of the band with Clover, Lipstick Red, and Wicker White, alternating colors. Repeat this pattern all the way around the top of the bucket. It will take three or four coats to cover.

3. Paint the band at the bottom of the bucket with Lipstick Red. It will take three or four coats to cover.

4. Add a thin line of Green Dark above the red band on the bottom.

5. Mix Green Umber + Green Dark (1:1). To paint the curlicues, thin the green mixture with water to an ink-like consistency and fill a #1 liner brush.

6. Using an old toothbrush, flyspeck the bucket with the same thinned green mix.

7. Paint the handle with Lipstick Red. Let dry and cure.

FINISHING

Varnish with several coats of high gloss or satin waterbase varnish. Let dry thoroughly. ❏

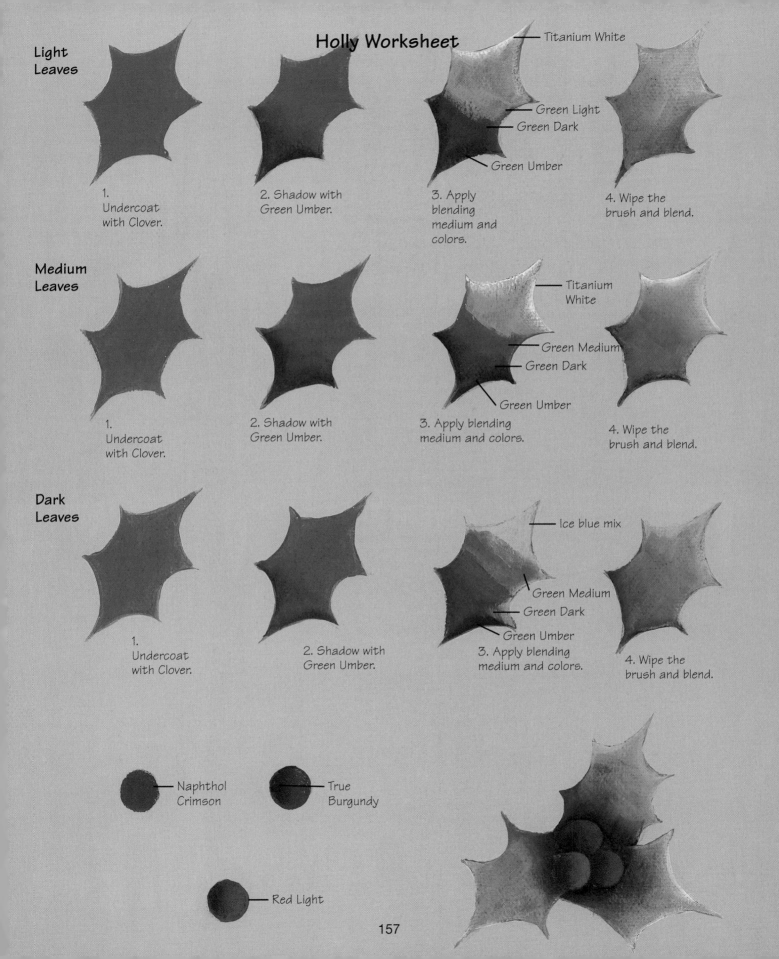

Holly Worksheet

Light Leaves

1. Undercoat with Clover.

2. Shadow with Green Umber.

3. Apply blending medium and colors.

- Titanium White
- Green Light
- Green Dark
- Green Umber

4. Wipe the brush and blend.

Medium Leaves

1. Undercoat with Clover.

2. Shadow with Green Umber.

3. Apply blending medium and colors.

- Titanium White
- Green Medium
- Green Dark
- Green Umber

4. Wipe the brush and blend.

Dark Leaves

1. Undercoat with Clover.

2. Shadow with Green Umber.

3. Apply blending medium and colors.

- Ice blue mix
- Green Medium
- Green Dark
- Green Umber

4. Wipe the brush and blend.

Naphthol Crimson

True Burgundy

Red Light

157

Ribbon Worksheet

Undercoat with
Wicker White.

Float Red Light and
Naphthol Crimson.

Shade with True
Burgundy.

METRIC CONVERSION CHART
INCHES TO MILLIMETERS AND CENTIMETERS

Inches	MM	CM		Yards	Meters
1/8	3	.3		1/8	.11
1/4	6	.6		1/4	.23
3/8	10	1.0		3/8	.34
1/2	13	1.3		1/2	.46
5/8	16	1.6		5/8	.57
3/4	19	1.9		3/4	.69
7/8	22	2.2		7/8	.80
1	25	2.5		1	.91
1-1/4	32	3.2		2	1.83
1-1/2	38	3.8		3	2.74
1-3/4	44	4.4		4	3.66
2	51	5.1		5	4.57
3	76	7.6		6	5.49
4	102	10.2		7	6.40
5	127	12.7		8	7.32
6	152	15.2		9	8.23
7	178	17.8		10	9.14
8	203	20.3			
9	229	22.9			
10	254	25.4			
11	279	27.9			
12	305	30.5			

INDEX

A

Acrylic craft paints 14, 31, 44, 48, 56, 64, 66, 72, 92, 98, 108, 118, 126, 135, 140, 146, 154

Artist pigment acrylic paints 14, 31, 48, 56, 64, 66, 72, 80, 92, 98, 108, 118, 126, 135, 140, 146, 154

B

Baby oil 80

Basecoat 13, 20

Bees 140, 142, 143, 144

Berries 148, 150, 156, 157

Birdcage 146, 148

Birdhouse 135

Blending 14, 27, 34, 36, 64, 65, 66, 68

Blending medium 14, 27, 31, 34, 36, 44, 48, 56, 58, 64, 65, 66, 68, 80, 86, 108, 110, 154

Blueberries 74, 76

Blueberries Chair & Table 11, 70, 72

Blueberries Ensemble 70, 72, 77, 78, 79

Brown paper bags 17, 29

Brush strokes 23, 24, 26

Brushes 16, 31, 44, 48, 56, 64, 72, 80, 92, 98, 108, 118, 126, 135, 140, 146, 154

Bucket 154

By the Sea Tray 126

C

Cabinet 31

Chair 70

Chalk 17, 18, 29, 136

Clock 135

Coat rack 54

Color wash, see "wash"

Consistency 20

Contrast 20

Coral 128, 131, 132

Cotton rags 17, 29

Cultivating fork 92, 93

Curing 20

Curlicues 23, 75, 109, 112, 136, 148

Continued on next page

INDEX

D

Distressing 13
Double loading 20, 22, 25, 64, 66, 110, 136
Dragonfly on Metal Ceiling Tile 43, 44, 46, 47

E

Eat, Drink & Bee Merry Plate 140

F

Ferns 116, 118, 119, 120, 121, 122, 123, 124, 125
Filbert brush 16, 24
Finishing 19, 33, 46, 51, 57, 66, 75, 93, 100, 109, 123, 128, 136, 142, 148, 156
Fish on a Tin Tub 48, 50, 52, 53
Flat brush 16, 22, 24, 25
Floating 14, 26, 59, 64, 65, 74, 75, 94, 99, 110, 143
Floating medium 14, 26, 56, 59
Flower pots 82, 86, 92, 93
Flyspecking 19, 56, 57, 92, 93, 98, 100, 108, 111, 113, 135, 136, 140, 142, 154, 156
Foam stamps 72, 74, 118, 146

G

Garden Window 80, 82, 83, 84, 85, 86, 87, 88, 89
Glass and tile medium 14, 80
Glazing medium 15, 26, 92, 98, 99, 118, 126, 128, 135, 140, 154
Gloves 92
Gold leaf 80, 83, 84
Graphite paper 17, 29

H

Headboard 96
Highlighting 26, 60, 61, 74, 94
Holly 154, 156
Holly Bucket 153, 154

I

Ink pen 98, 126
Inking 98, 99, 100, 128, 130, 131

L

Ladybug Garden Set 90, 95
Ladybugs 92, 94
Lamp 70
Latex wall paint 31
Leaf (leaves) 33, 34, 57, 64, 65, 74, 108, 148, 150
Leaf Bordered Picture Frame 66, 67, 68, 69
Lemon Kitchen Shelf 106, 108, 109, 110, 111, 112, 113, 114, 115
Lemons 108, 109, 110, 111, 113, 114, 115
Lilac Cabinet 31
Lilacs 33, 36, 37, 39
Line stroke 23
Liner brush 16, 23, 25
Loading the brush 21, 23

M

Masking tape 72, 92
Mediums 14
Metal ceiling tile 44
Metal primer 44
Moss 148, 150

O

Oil paints 80, 82, 83
Old Pieces 12, 13
Outlining 20

P

Paints 14
Palette 15
Palette knife 17, 29
Paper towels 17
Paste wax 18
Pearlizing medium 140, 143
Pencil 29
Picture frame 66
Plant stand 146, 148
Plate 140
Polliwog stroke 21
Preparing Your Projects 12
Pyracantha 148, 150
Pyracantha Birdcage & Plant Stand 146, 148, 152, 153

R

Ribbon 156, 158
Round brush 16, 21, 24
Rubbing alcohol 44, 80

S

Sandpaper 17, 29
Sea sponge 48, 51, 72, 74
Seashells 100, 101, 102, 103, 126, 128, 130, 132
Seashells Headboard 11, 96, 104, 105
Shelf 106
Shading 26, 60, 74, 99, 136
Sponge brush 18, 31, 44, 66, 72, 92, 98, 108, 118, 126, 135, 140, 146, 154, 156
Sponging 51, 74, 76
Spray sealer 72, 98, 126, 146
Springtime Birdhouse Clock 135
Squiggles 23
Stencil brush 20, 56, 59, 135, 136, 146, 148
Stippling 20, 56, 57, 59,

135, 136, 146, 148
Stylus 17, 29
Sunflower 57, 58, 59, 60, 61, 62, 63
Sunflowers Coat Rack 54
Supplies 14

T

Table 70, 116
Tack rag 17, 29
Teardrop stroke 21, 23
Textile medium 15, 92
Tin tub 48
Toothbrush 19, 56, 92, 93, 98, 108, 111, 135, 136, 140, 142, 154, 156
Tracing paper 17, 29
Transferring a design 17
Tray 126, 140
Turpentine 80

U

Undercoat 18, 34, 57, 60, 61, 64, 65, 74, 75, 86, 110, 136
Unfinished wood 13

V

Vinegar 44, 154

W

Wagon 90, 92, 93
Waterbase varnish 18, 31, 44, 48, 56, 66, 72, 80, 92, 98, 108, 118, 135, 140, 146, 154
Water basin 17, 29
Wash 20, 99, 126, 128, 130, 131
Wax paper 80
Window 80
Woodland Ferns Table 116
❏